FLEET AIR AR

THE ADMIRALTY ACCOUNT OF NAVAL AIR OPERATIONS   1/6 NET

FLEET AIR ARM

PREPARED FOR THE ADMIRALTY

BY THE MINISTRY OF INFORMATION

1943   His Majesty's Stationery Office, London

Contents

THE RISE OF NAVAL AIR POWER

THE EYES OF THE FLEET

STRIKING FORCE:
THE TORPEDO AIRCRAFT

ESCORT IN THE SKY: THE FIGHTERS

WHEN THE SERVICES COMBINE

There are many men and women in the Forces who would welcome a chance of reading this book. If you hand it in to the nearest Post Office, it will go to them.

Printed by C. Tinling & Co., Ltd.,
Liverpool, London and Prescot.

1. THE SWORDFISH STRIKE IN BOMBA BAY

"THIS attack, which achieved the phenomenal result of the destruction of four enemy ships with three torpedoes, was brilliantly conceived and most gallantly executed. The dash, initiative and co-operation displayed by the sub-flight concerned are typical of the spirit which animates the Fleet Air Arm squadrons of H.M.S. Eagle under the inspiring leadership of her Commanding Officer."

Thus wrote Admiral Sir Andrew Cunningham, K.C.B., D.S.O., Commander-in-Chief Mediterranean Fleet, in a despatch from his flagship, H.M.S. Warspite, to the Secretary of the Admiralty.

The sub-flight belonged to a Swordfish squadron which had disembarked to Dekheila airport when the aircraft-carrier Eagle (Captain A. R. M. Bridge, R.N.) was lying in Alexandria Harbour in August, 1940. After the squadron had been ashore a few days, Air Commodore R. Collishaw, Air Officer Commanding the Western Desert, applied for some torpedo-aircraft to help him deal with enemy shipping off the Libyan coast. He appreciated their potentialities the more because he had himself been a pilot in the Royal Naval Air Service during the last war, and later had served as Wing Commander in H.M.S. Courageous.

One of the squadron observers was accordingly sent as Naval Liaison Officer to Ma'aten Bagush, the headquarters of the Royal Air Force in the Western Desert. Next day three Swordfish followed, accompanied by an aged Victoria aircraft carrying the maintenance ratings and a conglomeration of tool-boxes, chocks, torpedo-gear and spare parts. The R.A.F. officers welcomed the pilots and observers, and the ground staff took the naval mechanics under their wing.

For the first few nights the sub-flight carried out anti-submarine patrols along the coast, without result. At 11 o'clock one evening the pilots were called to the Operations Room and told that the Blenheim dusk reconnaissance over Bomba Bay (between Tobruk and Benghazi) had reported a submarine depot-ship lying in the bay and a submarine heading in from seaward. Here was an ideal target for the torpedoes of the Swordfish. It was decided that the sub-flight should move up to Sidi Barrani next morning, re-fuel there, and await the report of the dawn reconnaissance.

Early next morning, 22nd August, Captain Oliver Patch, Royal Marines, arrived by air from Dekheila. As the senior officer he took command of the sub-flight, which flew off for Sidi Barrani, armed with torpedoes, at 7 a.m. And here a word of praise must be given to Leading Torpedoman Arthey, who, in the words of one of the pilots, "during a week of blowing sand, had nursed his charges with such loving care that they ran with the smoothness of birds when at length we dropped them."

After 90 minutes' flying, the Swordfish arrived over Sidi Barrani, which looked as though a tornado had passed over it. They succeeded in landing among the bomb craters without mishap. While the aircraft were refuelling, the crews were taken to the "Mess-cum-Ops Room," which one of them described as "a cunningly constructed edifice of petrol tins filled with sand, roofed by a tarpaulin, containing two wooden benches, a collection of camp stools, and an atmosphere of 85 per cent dust, 10 per cent tobacco smoke and 5 per cent air." There

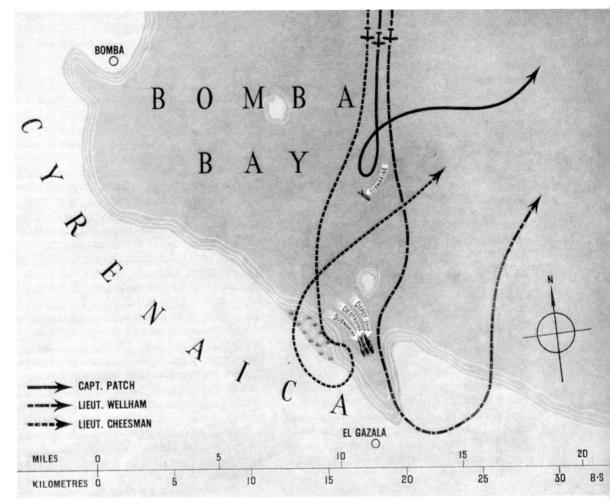

NEAT AS A PIN. In this attack in Bomba Bay, Libya, on 22nd August, 1940, a small striking force of Swordfish destroyed four enemy warships with three torpedoes. The submarine heading in from the sea was first to go. The aircraft on the right went on to sink the depot-ship lying at anchor. The second submarine was sunk by the remaining aircraft, and the explosion set fire to the destroyer in the middle.

they had a breakfast of tinned sausages, with the inevitable baked beans of the desert, and bread liberally covered with marmalade dug out of a 4-lb. tin with the breadknife.

The dawn reconnaissance showed that the targets were still in Bomba Bay. At 10.38 a.m. the sub-flight took off again and headed out to sea in V formation, led by Captain Patch.

As his observer and navigator, Captain Patch had Midshipman (A) C. J. Woodley, R.N.V.R., who, although he was suffering from tonsillitis, had insisted on taking part in the raid.

The Swordfish, flying low over the sea, shaped a course 50 miles from the coast, to avoid the attention of any prowling Italian fighters. At 12.30 they turned inshore and, thanks to Midshipman Woodley's accurate navigation, found themselves flying straight into Bomba Bay. They then opened out, fanwise, to about 200 yards. Four miles from the shore, in the centre of the bay, they sighted a large ocean-going submarine, dead ahead of the leader. She was steaming at about two knots on the surface, apparently charging her batteries. The crew's washing was hanging out to dry. Three miles beyond her, at the mouth of a creek known as An-el-Gazala, a cluster of shipping was visible.

As the striking force approached, now flying only 30 feet above the sea, the submarine opened up a vigorous but ineffective fire upon the starboard aircraft with her two .5 machine-guns. The rear guns of the port and starboard aircraft replied. Captain Patch turned swiftly to starboard, then smartly back to port, and dropped his torpedo from a range of 300 yards.

On seeing the splash of the torpedo those of the submarine's crew who were on deck jumped into the sea. A few seconds later the torpedo hit the submarine amidships, below the conning-tower. There was a loud explosion, followed by a cloud of thick black smoke. The submarine blew up in many pieces. When the smoke had cleared away, only a small part of her stern was visible above the surface.

Captain Patch, having completed his attack, turned out to sea again. The port and starboard aircraft, piloted by Lieutenant (A) J. W. G. Wellham, R.N., and Lieutenant (A) N. A. F. Cheesman, R.N., were now about a mile apart. They flew on towards the vessels lying inshore, which they identified as a depot-ship, a destroyer and another submarine, the destroyer being in the centre. The depot-ship opened fire with a few high-angle guns depressed along the surface. The destroyer joined in with her pom-poms and multiple machine-guns, and the submarine with her .5's. The fire was not concentrated, but a .5 bullet struck the bottom of the port aircraft, without wounding Lieutenant Wellham, however. He was not to discover the damage done to the aircraft until later.

The two Swordfish closed the ships. Lieutenant Wellham, with Petty Officer A. H. Marsh as his observer, dropped his torpedo on the starboard beam of the depot-ship. As Lieutenant Cheesman was preparing to attack the submarine his observer, Sub-Lieutenant (A) F. Stovin-Bradford, R.N., noticed that they were over shoal water and, just in time, saved his pilot from leaving the torpedo in the sand. Lieutenant Cheesman was forced to fly in to 350 yards in order to let go in deep water. He could see the torpedo running the full distance until it hit the submarine amidships. She exploded instantly and set fire to the destroyer. Three seconds later Lieutenant Wellham's torpedo hit the depot-ship below the bridge. She began to blaze furiously.

Both Swordfish turned away and headed for the sea, Lieutenant Cheesman making a right-hand circuit of the Italian fighter airfield at Gazala. He and his observer waved triumphantly to the airmen on the ground, but the enemy made no attempt to engage them. Then there was a terrific explosion astern. The magazine of the depot-ship had blown up. The three ships disappeared from sight in a cloud of steam and smoke.

Forty miles from the coast the two Swordfish sighted an Italian Cant Z 501 flying-boat above them, but it flew on towards Bomba without altering course. Shortly afterwards they made contact with their leader and reached Sidi Barrani at 3 p.m., having flown a total distance of 366 miles. Lieutenant Wellham's aircraft was found to be unserviceable : a bullet had smashed the extension to the main spar and knocked a dent in the petrol tank, fortunately without puncturing it. Lieutenant Wellham returned to Ma'aten Bagush in Captain Patch's aircraft. Midshipman Woodley was confined to sick quarters on completing his duty :

apparently it was considered dangerous for him to be out of doors.

Not unnaturally, the Operations Staff remained dubious about the crews' claim to have sunk four ships with three torpedoes, until the photographs of the reconnaissance Blenheim brought complete confirmation.

Captain Patch was awarded the D.S.O., and the other pilots and the observers were also decorated.

A few days after the raid the Italian Radio admitted the loss of four warships by " an overwhelming force of torpedo-bombers and motor torpedo-boats."

2. AIRFIELDS AFLOAT: THE CARRIERS

THE Swordfish might have attacked the Italian warships in Bomba Bay with equal success had they been flown from a carrier instead of from an airfield on land.

The torpedo aircraft has extended the striking power of a fleet by 200 miles, just as the reconnaissance aircraft has extended its vision. Surface vessels need fighter aircraft to protect them in an attack from the sky as much as they need destroyers to protect them from submarines, and naval aircraft remain instruments of sea warfare even when they operate from a shore base.

Naval officers have shown their eagerness to fly since the experimental days when the risks were by far the greatest. Among the earliest was Lieutenant (now Vice-Admiral) R. Bell Davies, who won the V.C., D.S.O and A.F.C. in the last war.

In the initial stages the Royal Flying Corps was responsible for both naval and military flying, but a month before the outbreak of war in 1914 the Naval Wing was transformed into the Royal Naval Air Service. By 1918 it had 3,000 aircraft, 5,000 officers and 50,000 men. During the war naval aircraft operated in the Dardanelles, the Mediterranean and East Africa ; squadrons were lent to the British Expeditionary Force in France, where they flew side by side with the pilots of the R.F.C., and naval airships proved their value on coastal reconnaissance and patrol. It was a naval pilot, Flight Sub-Lt. Warneford, who won the Victoria

Cross for destroying a German Zeppelin by bombing it from the air.

In April, 1918, the Royal Naval Air Service and the Royal Flying Corps were amalgamated to form the Royal Air Force, and for the next 20 years the Navy had no flying branch of its own. In 1924 a compromise was reached by the formation of the Fleet Air Arm of the Royal Air Force, which remained under the operational control of the Admiralty. The Admiralty provided 70 per cent of the pilots (including a certain number of officers from the Royal Marines), and all the observers and telegraphists. The Air Ministry built the Naval aircraft to Admiralty requirements and was responsible for administration and accommodation ashore, for training facilities, and for the balance of the pilots and all the maintenance staff. Since only officers with R.A.F. commissions were allowed to fly, the naval pilots had to hold two commissions.

This was a form of dual control which worked only through the good will of the officers and men of the two Services. Compromise is rarely satisfactory, and in 1938 it was decided that the Admiralty should have absolute control of its own Air Arm, with the necessary shore bases.

Later, Coastal Command was placed under the operational control of the Admiralty. That is the situation to-day : the Admiralty states the tasks that are to be carried out by coastal aircraft, whether they belong to the R.A.F. or to the Navy, and Coastal Command is responsible for translating plan into action. Ship-borne aircraft are at the disposal of the admiral of the force in which they form a unit.

The new organization came into official operation on 24th May, 1939, the Air Ministry having handed over to the Admiralty certain airfields, including that at Lee-on-Solent, which became the headquarters and barracks of the Fleet Air Arm ashore, styled H.M.S. Daedalus.

The Navy's chief difficulty was that although it had plenty of pilots, observers and telegraphists it had no maintenance ratings trained to the all-important work of servicing the aircraft. The problem was met by the Air Ministry allowing a certain number of volunteers to transfer to the Navy, and lending 1,500 senior air artificers, fitters and mechanics, many of whom, wearing R.A.F. uniform, are still doing valuable work with carrier-borne squadrons and at naval air stations ashore. At the same time the Navy began training its own body of maintenance ratings, who are gradually freeing the N.C.Os. of the R.A.F.

The member of the Board of Admiralty responsible for the provision of naval air equipment is the Fifth Sea Lord, under whom work the Director of Airfields and Carrier Requirements, the Director of Air Equipment, and the Director of Air Maintenance and Repair, who controls the servicing of the aircraft. On the Staff side the Assistant Chief of Naval Staff (Air) deals with naval air policy ; the Naval Air Warfare Division of the Naval Staff is responsible for tactics and

THE CARRIERS GROW UP. The Pegasus, *top*, first aircraft-carrier, served in the last war. She carried seaplanes only, lowering them and recovering them by crane. The Argus, *centre*, was the first carrier to have a full flight-deck and a lift, seen just for'ard of the Blackburn biplane, to take her aircraft down to the hangar. The Furious, *below*, drives through a heavy sea.

training, and decides the types of aircraft, weapons, and equipment required, and the Naval Air Organization Division deals with the daily running of the Fleet Air Arm machine. The Second Sea Lord's department is concerned with personnel. The function of the naval representatives of the Ministry of Aircraft Production is to ensure that the Admiralty's requirements in the design of naval aircraft and equipment are met.

Naval air stations at home are administered by two Admirals. The Flag Officer, Naval Air Stations (F.O.N.A.S.), delegates to a Rear-Admiral (R.A.N.A.S.) matters in connection with the northern stations, the chief of which is at Donibristle (H.M.S. Merlin) and dates back to the days of the Royal Naval Air Service. There are two naval air repair yards, which are the equivalent of naval dockyards, carrying out repairs and maintenance which cannot be done in the squadrons, and also modifying and issuing fresh aircraft. If a major crash comes in, a Board is held to decide whether the aircraft can be economically rebuilt or whether it should be " reduced to produce," when as much material as possible is salvaged, to be used in other aircraft. The administrative personnel is naval but the mechanics are civilians ; these " airyard mateys " include a large proportion of women.

During the war, naval air stations have expanded rapidly, not only in England and Scotland, but in the Middle East, in Africa, in the West Indies and in Ceylon. Every station bears the name of a commissioned ship and, true to the tradition of all naval shore establishments, the engaging fantasy of shipboard life is maintained.

Each has its own quarterdeck (usually a neatly-tended plot of grass with the White Ensign flying), the officers sleep in " cabins," mess in the " Ward Room " and " go ashore " when they leave the station. Orders are piped as at sea (the order for black-out is " Darken ship "), half-holidays are " make and mends " and when buses are provided to take the liberty men to the nearest town they become " liberty boats."

In such ways does the Navy show its wisdom and respect for time past ; and when young officers and ratings leave " the beach " to embark for the first time in a carrier they are not wholly unfamiliar with the speech and custom of life afloat.

Ships have been used for carrying aircraft since the early stages of the last war. The first aircraft to be taken in ships were on platforms built over the for'ard gun turret. The earliest flight from a ship at sea was made in 1912 from the battleship Hibernia, steaming at 12 knots, but at that time there was no means of landing back on the ship. The aircraft had to come down alongside and was hoisted inboard by a derrick, in much the same way as reconnaissance aircraft carried in battleships and cruisers are recovered to-day. The pioneer carrier was the old Ark Royal, later re-named Pegasus and still in service, which was laid down as a merchant ship but converted to carry aircraft before her launch. The fast cross-Channel packets Empress, Engadine and Riviera were fitted with hangars for seaplanes and with cranes for hoisting them into and out of the water. These vessels took part in the early bombing raids on Cuxhaven and Wilhelmshaven ; the Engadine flew off an aircraft at the Battle of Jutland, and towed the disabled battleship Warrior out of action. Torpedo-aircraft were first used in the Isle of Man packet Ben-my-Chree, and a number of capital ships carried their own aircraft, and were fitted with kite balloons for spotting during naval bombardments.

Then came the Campania, the Cunard record-breaker, which was converted as a carrier in 1916. Her for'ard funnel was replaced by two, set on either side of the ship, to make room for a runway built right down to the bows. Her seaplanes, mounted on light trolleys, flew down this runway and dropped the trolleys as they took the air. They still had to land in the sea, however. Sometimes they were recovered intact.

The next development was the Furious, the last of Lord Fisher's hush-hush cruisers. Her monstrous 18-inch for'ard gun was removed to make way for a hangar and a flight-deck. She was the first carrier to operate landplanes. Pilots began to devise methods of landing direct on to a carrier's deck and in August, 1917, Squadron-Commander Dunning succeeded in skidding his Sopwith Pup on to the flight-deck of the Furious. This was the first true deck-landing at sea. He repeated the experiment a few days later, went over the bows, and was killed.

A so-called "flying-on" deck was then fitted to the Furious, and a further improvement appeared in the following year, when a partially-built Italian liner, the Conte Rosso, was reborn as the Argus, with a flush flight-deck which extended almost the whole length of the ship. There were no funnels to embarrass the pilot, the smoke being carried away in ducts either side of the stern. She was the first carrier to be fitted with lifts to strike her aircraft to the hangars below, and although her slow speed was against her she was the most successful carrier to date.

The Hermes was the first ship to be specially designed as a carrier. She took 15 aircraft, but, like her forerunners, she was too slow : speed is essential to a carrier, both to create sufficient wind over the deck to operate aircraft, and also to enable her to regain station on the fleet after she has turned into wind for flying operations.

Then came the Eagle, which had been laid down as a battleship for Chile, the Almirante Cochrane. She was the first "island carrier," her two funnels, bridges and masts being shifted to the extreme starboard side. Until her end in August, 1942, she was one of the best-loved carriers in the Navy.

Later still the Furious, and her sister ships the Courageous and the Glorious, were transformed by clearing off the upper works and building two hangars, one above the other. It was in the Furious that the once-famous Perch Club was inaugurated, the qualification for membership being 100 deck-landings. The motto of the club was "Perchance." In peace-time the Furious was probably the hardest-worked ship in the Fleet and the Navy of to-day owes her much.

The last carrier to be launched before the war was the noble Ark Royal, the embodiment of all past experience of carrier construction. She could accommodate 60 aircraft in her three hangars, and had two lifts, accelerators for catapulting, an emergency crash barrier, and arrester wires which could be raised or lowered hydraulically to facilitate deck-landing.

An immense crowd was present at the launching of the Ark Royal and she received much publicity in the press. Nevertheless, in the years before the war the public knew singularly little of the Fleet Air Arm, or of the functions of aircraft-carriers. There is a story of an old lady who, wishing to know more, paid her shilling during Navy Week at Portsmouth in the summer of 1938 and went on board the Courageous. Having looked about the flight-deck in some bewilderment, she approached the Officer of the Watch, tapped him on the shoulder, and inquired, "Tell me, my man, do these things really fly ? "

The truth of that story is vouched for by the officer concerned, but even were it apocryphal it would symbolize the ignorance of many. In the Service itself there were officers who considered that the use of naval aircraft would be restricted to reconnaissance at sea.

Recent experience has shown that a naval force within range of shore-based enemy aircraft is doomed unless it has an escort in the sky, but that when protected by an air umbrella, either from land airfields or from carriers, it may pass through narrow seas. Even the best carrier-borne fighters, however, are at a disadvantage, since their base is less secure than an airfield ashore. Should their carrier be sunk while they are aboard, they must sink with her ; if they are in the air their floating airfield is gone.

That the aircraft-carrier is vulnerable cannot be denied. Her long flight-deck and her great over-water hull make her an attractive target for surface, air and sub-marine attack. For her protection she must rely upon her own aircraft, or those of her sister carriers, and upon the guns of the force in whose company she sails.

Since the outbreak of war the losses of British carriers have been heavy. On 3rd September, 1939, the Navy had eight carriers at sea. The Ark Royal and the Courageous were with the Home Fleet. The Glorious was in the Mediterranean, the Eagle on the China Station. The Furious was employed on deck-landing training in the Firth of Forth, and later on Atlantic convoy duty and ferrying aircraft. The Hermes was used first for operations against submarines in home waters, then for trade protection and raider-hunting in the South Atlantic. The Argus and the Albatross (an Australian-built seaplane carrier) were also in home waters; but the Argus was sub-sequently transferred to the Mediterranean for training duties and the Albatross to West Africa for trade protection.

The first loss was the Courageous, sunk by a submarine in September, 1939. The Glorious was sunk by enemy gunfire in June, 1940. These losses were replaced by the modern carriers Illustrious and Formidable. The Victorious was commissioned in May, 1941, but the Ark Royal was torpedoed in November of that year. The Indomitable appeared early in 1942. Japanese dive-bombers sank the Hermes off the coast of Ceylon in April, 1942, and the Eagle was

THE LAST WORD. Swift and powerful, the modern carrier Victorious steams to sea. Abaft her streamlined island are ranged some of her Albacore torpedo-bombers and on the extreme right a Fulmar fighter. The black shield for'ard is a wind barrier to protect the aircraft.

torpedoed while escorting a Malta convoy in August.

All these losses save the Ark Royal were old vessels, and the replacements were four new ships of 23,000 tons, so that, even apart from new Fleet carriers coming into commission, the Navy's strength in carriers is far greater than it was at the beginning of the war, in numbers, tonnage and accommodation for aircraft. With the commissioning of the new small escort carriers, it is increasing every month.

The Illustrious and her sister ships have a length of 750 feet and a beam of 95 feet, with islands stream-lined to prevent the wind spilling over on to the flight-deck and interfering with aircraft flying off and landing on. Their armament consists of 16 of the new 4·5 dual-purpose guns. Their complement is 1600, and their speed 31 knots. In January, 1942, the Illustrious survived a savage and continued dive-bombing attack while escorting a convoy to Malta ; although hit several times both at sea and while in harbour at Malta, she was able to proceed to Alexandria under her own steam.

The carriers' proper function is to operate with ships at sea beyond the range of enemy airfields, but the exigencies of war have frequently compelled their squadrons to be based ashore or to be used in a narrow sea, when their function is to establish air superiority over a sea lane within range of enemy bombers. This they have done with success, in spite of the numerical inferiority of their aircraft. As more carriers come into commission it will be possible to operate several in company, as in the Malta convoy of August, 1942, and in the recent operations off the North African coast. To this end the United States has been converting merchantmen into small escort carriers. A number of these, handed over under Lease-Lend, are now in service with the Royal Navy.

The first of these escort carriers to come into operation was the Avenger, which rendered gallant service the first time she was in action. She was lost in the following month. She was followed by the Biter, another merchant ship converted while building. The funnel is stowed away out of sight on the starboard side. The Chart Room and the Air Operations Room are on the main bridge below the flight deck, which is about 450 feet long.

These ships are built entirely in the United States, and contain scarcely any wood. Even the bunks, lockers, chairs and tables are made of steel. Unlike the British-built carriers, however, the flight deck is planked, which makes for quietness below. There is a single hangar, with a lift. The equipment includes a bacteriological laboratory, an X-ray apparatus, and a supply of drugs which a small hospital might envy. All this equipment is provided under Lease-Lend ; even the crockery in the Ward Room has the U.S. Naval anchor, and the silver is marked " U.S.N." The ratings' messing arrangements are on the cafeteria system in force in United States ships.

Speaking at the commissioning ceremony of one of these carriers, Rear-Admiral Marquand, U.S.N., said to the Commanding Officer and ship's company : " Flying the White Ensign of Great Britain, this American-built, American-converted vessel has come to be commissioned at this United States Navy Yard on Wallabout Bay, once the stronghold of the British forces in the War of Independence. More clearly than any words do these circumstances bespeak the unity of the United Nations—the pooling of resources and men and materials which will one day repay the destruction wrought by the deceit and inhumanity of our enemies."

As the months go by, more and more of these carriers are coming into commission, with others converted in the United Kingdom. They are quick to build and far less expensive than the big carriers. In one way they are a reversion to the small carrier of the early days, the little Engadine and her sister ships, but in the hitting power of their aircraft is the difference between the old armoured car and the modern tank.

3. THE AIRCRAFT OF THE FLEET

OF the aircraft in service with the Fleet Air Arm, most famous is the Fairey Swordfish biplane, with a Pegasus III (later XXX) 750 h.p. engine. The Swordfish went into service as a torpedo-bomber-reconnaissance (T.B.R.) aircraft in 1935. It has had many successes in all the functions allotted to it, and its manœuvrability has done much to compensate for its lack of speed. The war record of the homely " Stringbags " has been unsurpassed by any other type of aircraft, either in variety of use or in achievement.

Although not the—

Long lean monarchs of the sky
That pilots would be proud to fly

visualized by an idealistic Fleet Air Arm poet, nevertheless they have the affection of those who have flown them, or fly them still. Frequently they have had to face the strongest opposition the enemy could produce, but although they have known losses, those losses have been small in comparison with their achievement, and more than once the skill of their pilots has enabled them to evade enemies with three times their speed and to wound them in return. They are now in the evening (albeit prolonged) of their day and those who now fly the last of them take a savage pride in that.

After the Swordfish came the Fairey Albacore, a biplane somewhat greater in span and length, with a single 1,065 h.p. Bristol Taurus engine which gives it a slightly increased speed. Like the Swordfish, it has a fixed undercarriage, a fixed gun in front and a free gun in rear, and carries a crew of three : the pilot, the observer and the telegraphist-air-gunner. Its striking load, like that of the Swordfish, is one 18-inch torpedo or a 1,500-lb. bomb load.

The Albacore is, in its turn, being replaced by the Fairey Barracuda, a newer and faster torpedo monoplane with a single Merlin engine and an increased range, and also by the American Grumman Tarpon, a torpedo-aircraft which became famous in the Midway battle under its American name, Avenger It carries a 21-inch torpedo or a ton bomb-load, and has a speed (unofficial estimate) of 270 m.p.h.

The main operational role of the naval fighter aircraft is to give protection to a fleet or convoy, or to escort an air striking force. The Blackburn Skua, however, a two-seater fighter-dive-bomber, was also used for offence, particularly during the Norwegian campaign. Both the Skua and the Sea-Gladiator (the Navy's first multi-gun single-seater fighter biplane) were replaced by the Fairey Fulmar, a two-seater fighter with eight guns for'ard. The American Grumman Martlet, which came into service in 1940, is a single-seater fighter, faster than the Fulmar, with a cruising speed of 290 m.p.h., and equipped with four .5 machine-guns. It is a compact, tubby-looking aircraft, and

WITH THESE THEY SEARCH. The Walrus shown here is an amphibian used for spotter-reconnaissance, as were the smaller Seafox floatplanes now replaced by Kingfishers.

WITH THESE THEY STRIKE. The Swordfish, *above*, is a torpedo-bomber also used for spotting and reconnaissance. The Albacore, *below*, a later type than the Swordfish, is in turn being replaced by the Barracuda.

one pilot has described it as " a sweet machine to fly." The Royal Navy has cause to be grateful to the United States for providing these aircraft at a time when the need of a fast fighter was very great ; and the supply, begun before the United States entered the war, continued subsequently in increasing numbers. The Grumman Martlets are not only good aircraft, but, as these pages will show, British

WITH THESE THEY FIGHT. The Skua, *top left,* and the Fulmar, *bottom right,* have given way to the Martlet, *top right,* the Seafire, *centre,* an adaptation of the Spitfire. and the Sea-Hurricane converted from the Hurricane

naval pilots have made good use of them.

Carrier-borne aircraft suffer from certain limitations which until recently have restricted their speed and performance. The strong undercarriage, necessary for deck

landing, the folding wings, to allow for carriage in the lifts and stowage in the hangars, the tail-hooks and the strengthening of the fuselage to take the strain of the arrester-gear, together with increased armament, navigational instruments and wireless sets, all mean additional weight. Besides this, the wing-loading and landing speed must be kept low. These essentials affect the design, but the problems are being overcome, particularly in the latest types of naval fighters. The Hurricane I, which played so memorable a part in the Battle of Britain, was converted to the Sea-Hurricane by fitting a hook to engage the arrester-wires and equipment for catapulting when necessary. The Sea-Hurricanes particularly distinguished themselves in the Malta convoy of June, 1942, and since then the IIC type, armed with 20 mm. cannon, has come into service. The Seafire, a Spitfire type similarly converted, operated as carrier-borne aircraft for the first time in November, 1942.

The other types of aircraft in service with the Fleet are the spotter-reconnaissance amphibians and the light reconnaissance seaplanes which are mostly catapulted from battleships and cruisers. The most important is the Vickers' Supermarine Walrus, which has a record second only to the Swordfish. It came into service eight years ago and is the oldest type operating in the Fleet Air Arm. It is an improbable-looking aircraft, with its Pegasus III 750 h.p. " pusher " engine between the main planes, but in spite of its awkward appearance it can land on the sea as lightly as a seagull, and as it emerges from the water with its wheels down to climb the runway to its hangar ashore it resembles a sea-monster making for the land ; at sea it must taxi alongside its parent ship to be hoisted on board by a crane. The Walrus carries a pilot, an observer and a telegraphist-air-gunner. Its armament is one Lewis gun for'ard and one aft, and it has a normal endurance of about four hours. It operates independently and, although its functions are mainly spotting and reconnaissance, it can carry bombs and depth-charges.

A smaller type, the Seafox floatplane, now replaced by the American Kingfisher, did good work earlier in the war, notably at the Battle of the River Plate. Swordfish and Albacores can also be fitted with floats to allow them to be carried in battleships and cruisers.

4. WHEN A SAILOR LEARNS TO FLY

THE new carriers which are coming into commission, and the increasing number of naval squadrons afloat and ashore, demand a corresponding increase in pilots, observers and telegraphist-air-gunners and in maintenance ratings to keep the aircraft flying.

The officers of the Fleet Air Arm are naval officers who specialize in flying, just as others specialize in submarines. Among them are executive officers of the Royal Navy, the Royal Naval Reserve and the Royal Naval Volunteer Reserve, although executive Reserve officers are no longer allowed to specialize as pilots. A number of officers from the Royal Marines take up flying duties, retaining their own ranks and uniforms. The Air, or (A), branch of the Royal Navy contains many officers who have previously held commissions in the Royal Air Force or had experience of civil flying.

Since the introduction of the Armed Forces Act, direct entry has almost invariably been through the Lower Deck. Prospective candidates join as Naval Airmen II, the pilots and observers normally being commissioned in the (A) branch of the

PILOT   OBSERVER

R.N.V.R. on successful completion of training. On both arms these officers wear a small "A" within the loops of gold lace, and on the left arm only the pilot's or observer's wings. Thus the junior ranks of the Fleet Air Arm are to-day almost entirely filled by officers of the R.N.V.R. and the corresponding Dominion Services. The telegraphist-air-gunner is a rating; he becomes a Leading Naval Airman on completion of training, and wears the T.A.G.'s badge on his arm.

" When a sailor learns to fly," wrote Sir Walter Raleigh in *The War in the Air*, (1922), " he remains a sailor, and the air for him is merely the roof of the sea." This is still true of naval officers who specialize in flying, but to-day the majority of entries are young men, either straight from school or on the threshold of their careers, who have as little practical experience of the sea as they have of the sky, though some may have served in the Sea Cadet Corps or the Air Training Corps, many of whose squadrons are affiliated to naval air stations. They can join the Navy for flying duties through the " Y Scheme," under which Naval Selection Boards in various parts of the country recommend boys between the ages of 17 and 18 for training as pilots, observers and telegraphist-air-gunners.

Let us suppose that three school friends decide to apply for entry under this scheme— ordinary boys who have been to ordinary schools, where they have obtained the School Certificate. Let us call them Peters, Oliver and Green. They seize the opportunity which the Navy offers them of learning to fly and of going to sea at the same time.

Peters wants to be a pilot. He is alert, intelligent, with plenty of initiative. He is a hard-hitting batsman and a dashing three-quarter. He can drive a car and is fond of tinkering with its engine. He is a sound shot with a rifle.

Oliver is the cool, calculating type, who thinks well before he acts. He is the kind of steady batsman who can be relied upon to play the bowling when things have been going badly. His strong subject is maths. He has taken the trouble to find out the duties of a naval observer, and knows that they are no less important than the pilot's. He has learnt that the observer is responsible for the navigation of the aircraft, that during a reconnaissance he will act as the admiral's spy-glass and will be in charge of the aircraft during its bombing-run. All this attracts him, and he decides that he is better fitted to be an observer than a pilot.

Green is more of a plodder than either Peters or Oliver. Unlike them, he has never distinguished himself either at work or games, and his maths. are weak. But he has been popular with both masters and boys because of his honesty and reliability. He has no particular desire to be an officer but he does want to fight. He knows the high standard the Navy demands of its telegraphists and is prepared to learn. He determines to apply for entry as telegraphist-air-gunner.

The application forms are filled in and dispatched. The day comes when the three friends appear before the Selection Board. Peters is called in first. He is keyed up for the ordeal and tremendously excited, determined to do his best. As he is ushered into the room by a Wren he sees a long table at which are seated a Captain, R.N., an Instructor-Captain, and a Lieutenant who is wearing the pilot's badge. The President bids him good morning and asks him to sit down. He takes the chair opposite the President and awaits the attack.

He does not find the ordeal so terrifying as he had expected. It seems that the Board is not trying to bowl him out, but is sending down an over that will enable him to display his form. He answers the President's friendly

P.O. AIR MECHANIC
(Air Frames)

LEADING AIR FITTER
(Engines)

TELEGRAPHIST
AIR GUNNER

AIR GUNNER

queries about himself frankly and without trying to show off.

Then the Instructor-Captain takes a hand. By a few shrewd questions he is able to assess just how much trigonometry and maths. Peters really knows : no chance of stealing a quick run here. But the Instructor-Captain seems satisfied and then the President hands him a list of H.M. ships.

" Just tell me what you think they were called after," he says. " Take this one— Kenya."

" A British colony in East Africa, sir,"

" Right. And this one—Benbow ? "

" A British admiral, sir."

" Good," says the President. " We had someone in just now who said it was a public house."

After a few more questions to test Peters's history, geography, and general knowledge, the President pushes towards him some small ship models and asks him to identify them. Peters has a little trouble in distinguishing between a destroyer and a corvette, otherwise all goes well. The President then hands him over to the Fleet Air Arm representative.

Peters finds this young man more alarming than the senior officers. Why does he want to join the Navy ? Why does he want to be a pilot ? Does he know anything about motor cars and their engines ? What are the main types of naval aircraft ? Can he identify them ? Peters can, and does from the models on the table.

" What would you do if you were flying from London to Liverpool and your observer gave you a north-easterly course ? " is the next question.

" I should tell him to think again, sir."

" I should hope so ! "

Peters is then asked to withdraw. After a few apprehensive moments he is recalled.

" It's all right," the President tells him " We've decided to recommend you to be trained as a pilot. You will be put on the unpaid Reserve and you'll get your papers as soon as you are eighteen. Meanwhile, we should like you to go on with your training in the Sea Cadet Corps, the Air Training Corps or the Home Guard."

Peters promises to do this and retires elated.

Oliver and Green follow. The Instructor-Captain goes more deeply into Oliver's mathematical qualifications and the Fleet Air Arm representative asks Green a number of questions about morse and the armament of naval aircraft. Both boys satisfy the Board and are recommended in their turn.

Later Peters and Oliver are directed to join at the Royal Naval Barracks, Lee-on-Solent, Green at H.M.S. Royal Arthur. The weeks that follow are a period of adjustment from civilian to naval life. They are not altogether easy weeks, but they are full of interest. First comes the excitement of kitting up with square rig (as the seaman's uniform is called), and learning to wear it as befits a Naval Airman. Then comes a course of disciplinary training to introduce the new entries to naval life and to accustom them to handle weapons with confidence, interspersed with swimming, visits to the dockyard and to the hangars, and lectures on the history of naval flying by the former Commander of a famous carrier.

After a month's initial training they go to H.M.S. St. Vincent, another shore establishment, where they meet Green, who has been undergoing a similar course in H.M.S. Royal Arthur. They soon become sensible of the tradition by which the Navy, in its

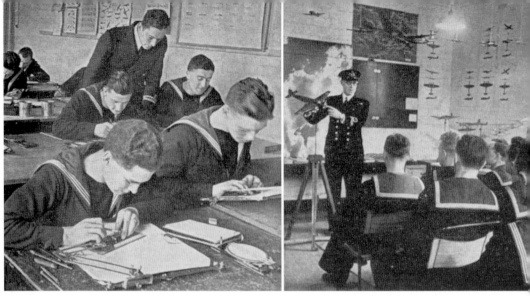

MUCH TO LEARN. Observers will have to bring their aircraft home across feature-less tracts of ocean to a moving airfield. They study navigation, *left*. All airmen must learn to recognize aircraft types, *right*. *Below*, machine-gun instruction.

wisdom, sets such store. The establishment was built in 1777. It is a dignified red-brick building, solid and forthright, with gracious proportions and the beauty of age. Behind the wrought iron gates are a vast parade ground and a quarter-deck.

Peters, Oliver and Green are told off to the separate courses for pilots, observers and telegraphist-air-gunners. Green's course deals mainly with the principles of air gunnery and naval signalling. In Oliver's course the emphasis is on signals and navigation, since he will be required to take his aircraft across vast tracts of sea without a landmark to help him, back to a floating aerodrome which is but a speck upon the ocean. Ship recognition is an important part of the training of all three. By means of a box with two peep-holes the pupils can see a number of models, changed every day, at different angles and in varying lights. And since naval airmen are expected to be seamen too, they must learn to box the compass, to take bearings and to understand the action of the wheel, the rudder, and the ship's head ; they are given an opportunity for practical boat work and have lectures on sea terms, ship routine, the functions of warships, and Service customs and ceremonies.

After two months' training Peters and Oliver pass out as Acting Leading Naval Airmen. Now their paths diverge. Peters goes to an R.A.F. station for his elementary flying training, Oliver to H.M.S. Excellent for his gunnery course, Green to a naval air gunnery school for instruction as a telegraphist.

When the Admiralty took over control of the Fleet Air Arm the Cabinet decided that the Royal Air Force should remain responsible for training naval pilots. Under a scheme recently inaugurated by Rear-Admiral John Towers, U.S.N., one of the pioneers of American naval flying, a number of British naval pilots receive their complete flying training in the United States at the great naval air stations of Gross Isle, Pensacola and Miami.

Some members of Peters's course go to the United States, others accompany him to a R.A.F. station which is devoted entirely to training naval pilots. A naval officer acts as liaison between the R.A.F. and the Navy, and gives lectures on naval subjects, but all the flying instruction is carried out by R.A.F. officers and sergeant pilots. It is the best that can be given, and the instructors feel an added responsibility for teaching the pilots of another Service.

Then Peters goes to Kingston, Ontario, for his service flying training. There he must make fresh adjustments : to climate, food, and the customs and speech of those about him. All this helps to widen his experience of life, and, besides the Canadians, he meets many other Dominion pilots, particularly New Zealanders, of whom increasing numbers are joining the Fleet Air Arm. At the end of a further period of training he passes out as a qualified pilot and returns to England as a Midshipman (A) R.N.V.R. Some of his friends return as Petty Officers ; others, who have passed the age of 20, as Acting Sub-Lieutenants (A) R.N.V.R.

Since leaving H.M.S. St. Vincent, Peters has been under the wing of the R.A.F., and now, after a period of leave, he goes to the Royal Naval College, Greenwich, where he is reminded that he is not only a naval pilot but a naval officer. There, working, eating and sleeping in those noble buildings which were once a Royal Palace, he learns to develop the officer-like qualities (or O.L.Q. as the Navy tersely calls them) which the Selection Board perceived to be latent in him. The atmosphere is wholly naval, and he would be insensitive indeed if he could not respond to the dignity of those stone colonnades, those old grey buildings, each named after one of the men who brought the Navy to greatness, to the gilded naval crowns on gates and lanterns, and to the beauty of the vast Painted Hall, where he dines at long tables lighted by gleaming silver candelabra, in company with W.R.N.S. cadets, some of whom will soon be carrying

out the duties of Staff Officers to the second-
line squadrons of the Fleet Air Arm.

At Greenwich Peters may meet his friend
Oliver, now also a Midshipman (A),
R.N.V.R., but with observer's wings on his
left sleeve. Over a beer in the Gun Room,
they compare experiences. Oliver, unlike
Peters, has remained in Great Britain. After
his gunnery course in H.M.S. Excellent
(another stronghold of naval tradition) he
was sent to a naval air station which was
once a civil airport, and is now styled H.M.S.
Raven. There he spent two months con-
centrating on visual signalling and wireless
telegraphy. At the end of the course some
of the pupils were sent to Trinidad (H.M.S.
Goshawk) to complete their observer's
training ; Oliver and the remainder went
to a station on the east coast of Scotland
known as H.M.S. Condor, where his principal
instruction was in reconnaissance and in
navigation as a means to that end. Soon
he went into the air on exercises in Swordfish
and Walruses. He learnt to find his way
about in the air without using landmarks,
relying on his skill in plotting and air
navigation. The early practices were over

the land, but little by little he became
accustomed to working over the sea, until
he was familiar with its changing moods of
wind and fog and cloud. He also had
practical experience in ship recognition, and
learnt to take air photographs, which were
processed by specially trained Wrens.

At length Oliver became a qualified
observer, a highly skilled navigator confident
of bringing his pilot into visual contact
with the enemy and capable of taking his
aircraft back across the sea to his carrier,
if need be in the dark ; competent indeed
to fulfil the postulates of the Fleet Air Arm
parody :

> If you can keep your track when all about you
> Are losing theirs and setting " mag " for " true,"
> If you can trust yourself when pilots doubt you
> And get back to the ship out of the blue ;
> If you can keep control of your dividers
> And Bigsworth board and Gosport tube and pad,
> Or listen to the wireless and the pilot
> Talking in unison—and not go mad . . .
> If you can fill the unforgiving minute
> With sixty seconds' worth of ground-speed run,
> Yours is the Air—and everything that's in it,
> And—what is more—you'll be an " O ", my son.

On leaving Greenwich, Oliver is ready to
go to a working-up squadron, but Peters
still has his specialist training to complete as
a T.B.R. pilot. If he were a fighter pilot
he would go to the Naval Air Fighter School
at H.M.S. Heron in Somerset. There the
course includes formation flying, cross-
country and cloud flying, section attacks on
other aircraft, spinning and aerobatics,
forced-landing practice, dog-fighting, dummy
deck-landing by day and night, radio
telephony and air gunnery. By means of
the cine-camera gun a pilot's marksmanship
can be assessed with great accuracy ; this
work is done by Wrens on the station.

In H.M.S. Heron the instructors are naval
pilots with recent operational experience,
and the psychological effect of being taught
by men whom the pupils can admire and
trust is very great. Equally great is the
responsibility these instructors bear, for the
future of the Fleet Air Arm, and it may

SOMETHING ELSE TO LEARN. A Swordfish
is catapulted. Cruisers and battleships in mid-
ocean use this method of launching their
reconnaissance and spotter aircraft.

well be the safety of the Fleet itself, is in their hands.

The essentials of a good naval fighter pilot are that he must be efficient in every phase of his job—interception, air-fighting, deck-landing and night flying, and since he will be flying single-seaters, he must learn to develop that extra sense of the fighter pilot which enables him to find his way by instinct, aided by R/T and his instruments. He must also show his ability as an officer on the ground, and must have dash, a sense of responsibility, integrity and self-discipline, and confidence in himself. That he must have courage goes without saying ; but, as General MacArthur has said, courage alone and the willingness to die is not enough, for he needs the best weapons that can be procured and the skill to use them.

Pilots who are not being trained to fly fighter or T.B.R. aircraft go on their return from Canada to a naval air station for seaplanes on the South coast. It was once the headquarters of a motor yacht club and is the most luxurious air station in the Navy. Having received their elementary training in flying Walruses and Kingfishers, they proceed to another station on the Welsh coast, where they carry out spot landings on the water, landings alongside a ship, rough sea landings, and landings in the " slick "—the calm water left by a ship turning at speed in bad weather, which " irons out " the sea—and practise dropping bombs and depth-charges. They finish their training with a spell on board the veteran H.M.S. Pegasus for catapult work and recovery.

The pilots and observers of amphibians or of light reconnaissance floatplanes carried in battleships and cruisers are more closely identified with the life of the ship than they would be in a carrier, so that they must have a sound knowledge of naval routine and procedure. The pilot must also be able to handle his aircraft on the water as well as in the air. On one occasion a Walrus got lost while on reconnaissance from a cruiser off Freetown. When the fuel gave out the pilot forced-landed on the sea. He and the observer hoisted a parachute between the upper and lower main planes and ran before the wind for two days. An off-shore breeze made further progress towards land impossible, so they took to their rubber dinghy, sank the Walrus, and were eventually picked up by a native boat which took them to Freetown.

After completing his training the Walrus pilot goes to a pool unit on the east coast of Scotland, and while waiting to be posted to a ship carrying catapult aircraft he flies the observers under training in H.M.S. Condor, to which the seaplane station is a tender. The officers live in a requisitioned hotel, and the maintenance ratings' quarters are in an old factory, where they sling their hammocks and share the galleys, canteen and washrooms with the ratings of a submarine depot.

On leaving Greenwich Peters steers a different course from his fighter and Walrus pilot friends and goes for his torpedo training to a naval air station, H.M.S. Jackdaw, not far from H.M.S. Condor, in the Firth of Forth.

When he was at Lee-on-Solent it may be that he noticed the following maxim printed on the wall of the Torpedo Office :

" Their want of practice will make them unskilful, and their want of skill, timid. Maritime skill, like skill of other kinds, is not cultivated by the way, or at chance times."

It was Thucydides who wrote that, two thousand years ago, but Peters is soon to find that its application is as true to-day, for in no branch of naval flying is more skill and practice required than in dropping torpedoes.

He begins his training by low flying over the sea, taking off and landing with a dummy torpedo, then practises aiming, going through the methods of attack without dropping. After he has been in the target ship to watch the instructors giving a demonstration he goes up in a sub-flight, led by an instructor, to drop dummies, then live torpedoes, or runners as they are called. The final stage

is the squadron attack, when the sub-flight circle round the target ship above the clouds, dive steeply into position for the attack to within 50 feet of the sea, drop their "fish," and take avoiding action as they turn away, while the recorders in the target ship watch the track of the torpedoes, which have been set to pass underneath and aimed astern of the ship. The results of these attacks are analysed by Wrens.

Having completed his torpedo training Peters goes on to H.M.S. Peewit for a course in deck-landing, by day and by night A stretch of the station run-way is marked out to represent a carrier's flight-deck—but is made much longer, since the dummy deck on the airfield is stationary whereas the carrier would be creating a wind by her

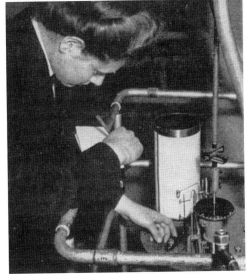

WRENS PLAY THEIR PART. *Above,* Wren Armourers service a Browning. *Below,* They keep weather records. This Wren reads the anemometer, the instrument that records wind strength and direction *Left,* " Spilling " a parachute.

forward speed—and is marked by hooded lights at night: The main object of the exercise, which is known as " circuits and bumps," is to teach the pilot the standard approach to land on a carrier in such a way that his hook will catch one of the arrester-wires stretched across the tarmac and, above all, to put complete confidence in the Deck-Landing Control Officer, on whom his life and the safety of his aircraft will depend once he is at sea.

The Deck-Landing Control Officer is known as " the Batsman "—from the implements with which he signals to the pilots. These are illuminated at night, and the incoming aircraft switches on three small lights to show its position and altitude. " Go slower "—" Go lower "—" A little to your right "—" Steady as you go," and finally, as the bats are swept together, " Cut your engine." The pilot closes his throttle and if he has obeyed the signals he will not fail to make a correct landing.

When Peters has finished his deck-landing course he is a fully trained T.B.R. pilot and is posted to a squadron, possibly one that is working up at H.M.S. Landrail, an air station on the west coast of Scotland. There, it may be, he meets Oliver again, and also Green, who by this time is a fully-fledged telegraphist-air-gunner.

Green has had to work as hard as either of his friends. On leaving H.M.S. St. Vincent he went to one of the air stations which the Admiralty took over from the R.A.F., now called H.M.S. Kestrel. It is an attractive station, with neat paths and well-kept flower beds. There he found some 300 air-gunners in various stages of training, some of whom, like himself, had joined through the Y Scheme, others from sea. They came from all walks of life and in his own course were a butcher's boy, a printer, an insurance clerk, a racing motorist's mechanic, a house-decorator, a farmer, a policeman, a brick-layer, a stable lad, a carpet salesman, a glassmaker, and a ripper in a paper mill.

With these companions Green spent 13 weeks in signals and wireless training, then went to an air station on the Cornish coast, H.M.S. Vulture, for air-gunnery. Having learnt the mechanics of naval aircraft armament and having fired on a ground range at a silhouette target of a Messerschmitt, he went into the air, first firing splashes in the sea, then carried out attacks on sleeve targets, cones of cloth 20 feet long streamed about 100 yards on a fine wire by a towing aircraft. When the exercise is over the sleeve is dropped on the ground and Wrens assess the number of hits. Should the target fall outside the station a reward of five shillings is paid for its recovery, an inducement which keeps the small boys of the village on the alert.

As on most naval air stations, Wrens also undertake much of the maintenance of the guns, and there is a small station nearby, used as an emergency landing-ground, which is entirely staffed by Wrens of the Fleet Air Arm, under a Wren officer, with a V.A.D. When the training squadrons are firing on the sea ranges the Wrens assess the hits and report to headquarters by telephone. They are also in charge of the bombing ranges used by the working-up squadrons, marking and sighting the bombs dropped on the targets. The only man in this Amazonian community is the elderly driver of the crash tender (or " blood waggon "), which is too heavy for the girls to start. He lives ashore.

Wrens play an important part, too, in the telegraphist-air-gunner's W/T training, as Green found when he returned to H.M.S. Kestrel for the second part of his course.

After practice in handling the receiver and transmitter sets he was sent to a hut on the perimeter of the airfield, where he began communication with an external ground station, working independently, and later in an aircraft on the ground. At last he went into the air, and learnt to ignore the noise of the engine and the slip-stream : a matter of practice, just as in a factory, where old hands can talk easily when a newcomer can hear nothing. On reconnaissance exercises he learnt to send his signals in code, the pilot telling him the substance of the information to be passed. The Wren W/T operators received and corrected these signals, so that Green was able to check his work when he reached the ground.

The Navy demands of its telegraphist-air-gunners an extremely high standard in wireless telegraphy. On an extended search there may be only one aircraft to spot the enemy,

OLD HANDS NOW

so that everything may depend on the report of a single man. Carelessness is the unforgivable sin and the highest tribute a T.A.G. can receive is for the Training Commander to report him as " reliable."

When Green has passed out he may look forward to rising to Warrant or even Commissioned rank. In this war the air-gunners have a fine record. Here is one example of their calm courage. On Easter Sunday, 1942, one of H.M.S. Indomitable's Albacores was searching for the Japanese fleet in the Indian Ocean and was attacked by a Mitsubishi 96. The air-gunner, a Yorkshireman, was hit in the arm but continued to fire his gun, then made his signal and got out his sighting reports. Having driven off the enemy aircraft he extracted the bullet from his arm with a screw-driver, put it in his pocket saying, " Must keep that as a souvenir," and then fainted from loss of blood while the observer was applying first aid.

THE GREAT DAY.   Landing on a carrier after shore training is finished is a great moment.
The Deck-Landing Control Officer guides the Seafire pilot in with his "bats."

5.   "THOSE IN WHOSE WORK THEY TRUST"

In H.M.S. Landrail, Peters, Oliver and Green learn for the first time the comradeship of an air squadron. They are no longer individuals but work as one company, each member of which is dependent on the other, and thus they come to understand that the best results are achieved not by the most efficient pilot, observer or air-gunner, but by the most efficient crew with good teamwork, and that a squadron commander can make a happy squadron as surely as an experienced commanding officer can make a happy ship, if he receives the support and co-operation of his men.

They also learn that every officer has his own part in the organization of the squadron. One—the senior pilot—is responsible for the maintenance of the aircraft, others for personnel, stores, armament, wireless equipment and parachutes. A squadron officer acts as staff officer and the senior observer attends to the welfare of the air-gunners. Once again they come to appreciate the services of the Wrens, who pack the parachutes and aircraft dinghies, fit the wireless equipment into the aircraft, service the guns, help to provide met. reports and check the aircraft parts when the squadron moves from one station to another, besides driving transport vehicles, cooking, waiting at table and acting as officers' stewardesses.

Flying together in the same Albacore the three friends practise mock torpedo and bombing attacks on targets at sea. Then the squadron may go to one of the Coastal Command stations for a short time as a "lodger unit" for minelaying, attacks on enemy shipping or anti-submarine work. The squadron has its own office and an allotted area in the station, the officers and ratings messing with the R.A.F. Relations between the two Services are excellent, and each learns to understand something of the other's work.

At last comes the day to which all the members of the squadron have been looking forward : they fly off to join an aircraft carrier. Peters' training in H.M.S. Peewit enables him to land his Albacore neatly on the flight-deck. The carrier spends some days exercising her aircraft in home waters, and it is not long before Peters and his companions become familiar with the procedure of flying at sea.

When the pipe for ranging aircraft is sounded over the ship's broadcaster the Albacores come up in the lift with wings still folded. The "pin-party" of seamen push them into position on the flight-deck and the maintenance crews spread the wings. Green, Oliver and Peters, wearing their "Mae Wests," climb into their places, and the squadron air mechanics help them into their harness. Peters starts up his engine. The Petty Officer in charge of the flight reports all correct to the Deck Officer, who gives the signal to the Commander (Flying). This officer, known as "Wings," is looking down on the flight-deck from his own bridge on the island, in close contact with the Captain, who is on the compass platform. The ship begins to turn into the wind. The Deck Officer brings the leading aircraft into

PERFECT LANDING. *Top.* The aircraft, this time a Martlet, is about to touch down on the rain-swept deck, while an asbestos-clad fire-fighter stands at his post. *Centre.* With its wings folded back, the aircraft is struck down into the hangar. *Below.* Looking down into the lift shaft. The big wedges lying on the wings are the chocks used on deck to brake the aircraft's wheels until the signal "Chocks Away" is given and the aircraft takes off.

position for the take-off by signalling to the pilot with a pair of small coloured flags. As soon as it has taxied into position, the " stop " signal is given, and the ratings who are handling the chocks place them at the wheels to prevent the aircraft from moving.

When the steam jet at the fore end of the flight-deck shows that the ship is steaming into the wind, Commander (Flying) shows a green flag, the executive signal for flying off. The Deck Officer signals " Chocks away." The leader takes off. When Peters' turn comes he holds the Albacore by the brakes until he sees the Deck Officer drop his green flag, and then flies off. The remainder of the flight follows at intervals of ten seconds and forms up on the bow of the ship.

Having taken part in an exercise with some of the carrier's fighters Peters receives a signal to return. The flight goes to the waiting position, a mile astern of the ship. The squadron distinguishing flag is shown at Number One port signal boom. The first sub-flight then closes the ship. Peters prepares for landing by lowering his hook, then circles round the ship, awaiting his turn to approach the deck.

When Commander (Flying) is ready he orders the affirmative flag, a white cross on a red ground, to be hoisted at Number Two port boom. From now onwards Peters is under the orders of the Deck-Landing Officer, who brings him to the right height and speed over the after end of the flight-deck. Peters has " backed up " the aircraft ahead so that there will be no delay : a high rate of landing is necessary for the efficient operation of the ship, which in action might be in her most vulnerable position. When he receives the signal to come on he makes a straight approach, with plenty of engine, nose well up, the aircraft hanging on its propeller and sinking steadily towards the deck. As he comes down his hook catches one of the arrester-wires and the Albacore comes to rest. Ratings run out to disengage the hook, the safety barrier is lowered and Peters taxies forward ; then the barrier is raised again for the next arrival, which touches down twenty seconds later. As Peters applies his brakes at

"TILL THE JOB'S DONE." These are some of the men whose trust it is to keep the aircraft in perfect flying and fighting order. *Below, left*, armourers at work on a Sea Hurricane's guns. *Above, left*, a group of Hurricanes is fuelled. *Right*, torpedomen.

the far end of the flight-deck the pin-party pounces on the Albacore, folds its wings, and parks it to await its turn to be struck down to the hangar, where it is tucked away with neatness and despatch, ready to be serviced by the squadron maintenance ratings.

In the days that follow, Peters and his comrades come to appreciate the work of these maintenance ratings as they never did ashore. There is a prayer used in the Fleet Air Arm which begins :

" Almighty God, Who makest the clouds Thy chariot and Who walkest upon the wings of the wind, we commend to Thy Fatherly protection all who ride the skies in the service of the Fleet, and those in whose work they trust."

The Fleet Air Arm is like an iceberg : the part seen rising to the sky is but a small proportion of the whole, and to maintain the pilots, observers and gunners in the air there is, working in the hangar below, a body of men upon whose skill and integrity the air crews' lives depend.

Among the senior rates are skilled Air Artificers, and there are some Flight Sergeants

still on loan from the R.A.F., but many of the air fitters and most of the air mechanics began the war as civilians and are enlisted for hostilities only. These men now join at a New Entry Training Establishment in the Midlands, fitly styled H.M.S. Gosling. There they are kitted up and pass through a ten weeks' course which will fit them to defend their airfield or their ship, for the Navy requires that, besides being technicians, they shall also be combatants, like every rating. At the end of this course they go on with their technical training elsewhere.

In the Navy there are four categories of air fitter and air mechanic : (A), who are responsible for airframes and rigging, the general assembly workers, trained as sheet metal workers, welders and joiners ; (E), the engine mechanics and machine operatives ; (L), the electricians, in whose care are all the complicated electrical fittings of the modern aircraft, including the maintenance of the camera guns, and (O), the men who service the ordnance, or armament, of the aircraft, including all bombing equipment.

The air fitters are skilled tradesmen who

have had over two years' experience in the engineering industry before they join. They are accepted on passing a trade test and wear fore-and-aft rig—jacket and peaked cap. The air mechanics, who wear square rig, need not have any previous trade experience, which is considered less important than an aptitude for the work to which their natural ability can be harnessed. Among them are grocers and butchers, and recently a costing clerk, with no mechanical knowledge when he joined, passed out top of his course. While they are in H.M.S. Gosling every attempt is made to fit the right man into the category most suited to him, by means of psychological tests and also by the personal observation of his work.

Most air fitters and air mechanics go from H.M.S. Gosling to R.A.F. training establishments, where there are naval sections, with naval officers in charge. The men work beside the R.A.F. mechanics under training, and the instructors are R.A.F. non-commissioned officers. The naval ratings live in their own hutments, however, have their own band, and their section of the station may be recognized by the washing that is hanging out to dry, for while at H.M.S. Gosling they have been taught, as every seaman is, to wash their own clothes.

The remainder go to a naval air training establishment, known as H.M.S. Daedalus II, at a market town in the midst of the pottery country. It was originally situated at Lympne, but in May, 1940, was moved at short notice when the R.A.F. required the station after the collapse of France. The establishment, which is a triumph of ingenious administration, is dispersed in thirteen different buildings in the town.

After about six months' training here both fitters and mechanics qualify at a naval air station as competent to give a certificate of airworthiness for aircraft and then may be drafted to a carrier.

Radio mechanics, including Wrens, are trained to test, maintain and repair all the radio apparatus in naval aircraft. The Navy has also begun to train a number of Wrens to relieve a proportion of the male air mechanics, (A), (E), (L) and (O), in shore-based squadrons at home and abroad. Their training is exactly similar to that of the men, and is carried out mainly at R.A.F. stations, although some go to H.M.S. Daedalus II, which is also responsible for the main instruction of the air apprentices, who are, in wartime, the only long-service maintenance personnel under training.

These boys, who are required to pass a preliminary examination, are called up from school after the age of fifteen. They are kitted up at an establishment (formerly a well-known preparatory school) near Lee-on-Solent. They spend three weeks on a course which includes drill, route marches, firing on the range, swimming, lectures on naval history, and visits to the workshops at Lee. Whenever possible they are taken for a flight.

They then pass on for a year's training in one of two preliminary training establishments, and go on for their special training in their own categories to H.M.S. Daedalus II, where they remain two years. They are grouped in four divisions, each with a Divisional Officer, a Chief Petty Officer, a Gunner's Mate (for drill) and P.T. instructors. The Chief Petty Officer is not an instructor but supervises their clothing and looks after their general welfare ; the boys are encouraged to go to him with their sorrows and their jubilations. From the senior divisions C.P.O. and P.O. apprentices are appointed, receiving a small increment of pay and being given jobs which are equivalent to those of the Leading Seaman of a mess deck. They are, in fact, in the position of prefects, and the wise policy of the Navy is to give them as much responsibility as they can shoulder.

The apprentices live and work apart from the fitters and mechanics. They have their own canteen and gymnasium, which can be used as a cinema. Each boy knows that he has the right to put his case or to receive help, and he is trained to trust those who teach him. If he is slack at his work he receives a " Captain's warning," and his parents are informed. If he fails to improve he may be discharged, but only after Admiralty sanction has been obtained. No boy has ever been suspended for misbehaviour only. The Navy trains him to behave.

At the end of three years the apprentices have a final technical examination and a trade test, then go to Lee-on-Solent to be rated, and spend a further six months " under report " in the squadrons and workshops of a naval air station, including brief courses at makers' factories, to emerge after further operational experience at the age of 20—21 as qualified air artificers, the most highly trained technicians of the Fleet Air Arm.

The care that is being spent on these young men's training is only beginning to bear fruit. Meanwhile the Navy has cause to be grateful not only to the R.A.F. men on loan but also to its own air artificers, fitters and mechanics who have borne the burden of over three years of war.

The maintenance staff's duty in action at sea is to get all the aircraft serviced and repaired as soon as possible, so that they may go into the sky again. Many has been the time when they have worked for three days and nights patching bullet holes, changing engines, and doing in a few hours jobs that might have taken a week ashore. As soon as an aircraft returns to the ship damaged, the staff of the carrier's workshop gets it down from the exposed flight-deck and sets to work on it within ten minutes of its having landed on. It may have had the propeller damaged, or it may need new wings, new wheels, patches on the fuselage or the planes—metal to be riveted in Fulmars and Martlets, fabric patches for Swordfish and Albacores. On one occasion a complete undercarriage was manufactured on board.

" The Fleet Air Arm never worry about the hours," said a maintenance rating in the Victorious after the Malta convoy of August, 1942. " They just work on till the job's done."

That is what their training teaches them to do, and such is the work of those in whom the air crews trust

ALL CORRECT. This is the scene upon which the Commander (Flying) looks down from his bridge the scene up to which all the intensive training and practised teamwork of the Fleet Air Arm leads

THE EYES OF TH

FLEET

6. FRIGATES OF THE AIR

RECONNAISSANCE was the earliest duty of naval aircraft, and remains one of their most important functions to-day. On reconnaissance responsibility falls heaviest upon the observer, for then he must be master of all the lessons he has learnt during his long training. He needs a practised eye, an acute mind and a resolute spirit. He must not only see clearly but appreciate the significance of what he sees and must be able to describe it with precision, conscious that on his report the admiral may act. Thus he may make or mar a battle. He is as essential to the modern fleet as were the frigates of Nelson's day ; had Nelson been able to catapault an aircraft from the Victory there would have been no need for him to search the Mediterranean for the French fleet, or to follow Villeneuve in the long pursuit across the Atlantic to the West Indies and back again.

Naval reconnaissance aircraft have not altered the principles of sea warfare, but they have vastly enlarged its scope. Their primary duty is to find and fix. Reports concerning the enemy may come in from many sources : from the R.A.F., from naval ships operating independently, from merchant ships, or from Admiralty intelligence. Flying to a range of 200 miles from the Fleet, the reconnaissance aircraft investigates such reports, or searches out enemy ships to plot and report them with precision. Raiders at large may entail months of continuous ocean search, as in the hunt for the Admiral Graf Spee, or a more intensive form of reconnaissance for a short period, as when the Swordfish of the Ark Royal were searching for the Bismarck, or those of the Formidable for the Italian fleet before the Battle of Matapan. Having found the enemy at a distance it is the duty of the aircraft and that of its reliefs to keep continuous touch until the enemy is no longer within air range.

Nor is this the only duty of reconnaissance aircraft. In the first months of the war, when magnetic mines were causing the Admiralty grave anxiety, naval observers, on account of their navigational experience, were attached to R.A.F. flights which had been equipped with devices for minesweeping, and operated off the coast of England and Egypt. Naval aircraft have reconnoitred enemy harbours, and the photographs they have secured, both before and after an attack, have proved of great value. They have found and reported the position of British convoys and outlying naval units and by passing orders to them by visual signals have enabled the Fleet to preserve wireless silence. They also carry out close search and anti-submarine patrols ahead of the Fleet from dawn to dusk, and when the Fleet is in harbour maintain daylight and moonlight searches to seaward from shore bases. For many months Walruses from H.M.S. Albatross were employed off Freetown on anti-submarine patrols and convoy escort duties.

This is a defensive duty, but in the first weeks of the war, before it was possible to put the convoy system into full operation, Swordfish and Skuas from the Ark Royal, the Courageous and the Hermes were employed offensively to hunt U-boats in home waters. While one or two aircraft patrolled ahead of the carrier, a striking force was kept in readiness to attack any U-boat reported. They sighted and attacked a number of U-boats, and their watchfulness undoubtedly forced the submarines down during this critical period. The carriers faced grave risks, however. The Ark Royal had a narrow escape from being torpedoed on 14th September, 1939, and the Courageous was sunk three days later. The Admiralty then decided that aircraft-carriers were too valuable to be risked in U-boat areas when the work could be done equally well by shore-based aircraft co-operating with anti-submarine vessels.

After the Admiralty's decision to withdraw carriers from submarine hunting, several were engaged in the interception of enemy raiders and merchant vessels. While the German pocket-battleship Admiral Graf Spee was at large, the Ark Royal was searching for her in the South Atlantic, the Eagle in the Indian Ocean. The Ark Royal's aircraft missed her by only a narrow margin. In their daily searches—arduous, monotonous and unspectacular—they covered millions of square miles and contributed to her being brought to action off the River Plate. The Glorious was also employed on trade protection in the Indian Ocean and the Hermes on the convoy route to Dakar, in co-operation with French naval forces.

During this period a number of German merchant ships were intercepted, including S.S. Uhenfels, loaded with a rich cargo of opium, by the aircraft of the Ark Royal. Catapult aircraft from the cruisers operating independently on the trade routes also made their contribution. Among others, the Shropshire's aircraft found S.S. Adolf Leonhardt, which was scuttled and abandoned.

In March, 1941, the Ark Royal's Swordfish intercepted the British ships San Casimiro and Bianca, which had been captured by the Scharnhorst and Gneisenau. They, too, were scuttled, but H.M.S. Renown took off the imprisoned British crews and the German prize crews, and landed them at Gibraltar.

While the Scharnhorst and Gneisenau were still preying upon merchant shipping in the Atlantic the Swordfish floatplane from H.M.S. Malaya, piloted by Lieutenant G. R. Brown, D.S.C., R.N., sighted them on reconnaissance during the afternoon of 8th March, 1941. The Malaya was then escorting a north-bound convoy from Sierra Leone and was between the Canaries and the Cape Verde Islands. The speed of the German warships, which turned away as the Malaya prepared to open fire at long range, made it impossible to bring them to action before dark and the Swordfish was accordingly ordered to return to the ship.

At 6.21 p.m. the Swordfish reported that it could not find the ship owing to the decreased visibility and the failing light. The Commanding Officer of H.M.S. Malaya (Captain, now Rear-Admiral, A. F. E. Palliser, D.S.C., R.N.) was then placed in

DAWN PATROL. A Walrus is catapulted from its parent ship to search the ocean.

a grave dilemma. A submarine was suspected to be shadowing the convoy (five ships had been torpedoed on the previous night) and the two enemy battle-cruisers, capable of high speed, were within 50 miles. To give the Swordfish a bearing might divulge the position of the convoy and enable the enemy to creep up and attack during the night. On the other hand, if he maintained wireless silence his aircraft would have to make a forced landing in the dark, with little prospect of being picked up. For a time he waited, hoping that the Swordfish might still find the ship. At last, as there was no sign of it, he authorized the transmission of two D.F. bearings, without using call signs. An Aldis lamp was shone skywards in the direction of the last position given by the Swordfish, and lights were shown through the roofs of the gun turrets. At 7.38 the Swordfish made a signal " Landing any minute now." That meant that its endurance was nearly at an end. There was still no knowing if it would find the ship in time. A little later it signalled " Good luck—cannot find you." Then the final words " Forced landing."

All that night the Swordfish lay helpless, breasting the Atlantic swell like a gull. But the crew kept it afloat and next morning those in the Malaya heard it sending out distress signals. The Malaya, with the convoy in her charge, could do nothing, but the signals were picked up by the Spanish ship Cabo de Buena Esperanza and by the Alfonso Perez, a Portuguese. On being asked to give his call sign the telegraphist-air-gunner, Petty Officer R. H. George, suggested replying " Aircraft belonging to H.M.S. Valiant "—to avoid disclosing the whereabouts of the Malaya. Both the neutral ships searched for many hours and at 8.42 that evening the Malaya intercepted a message from the Cabo de Buena Esperanza stating that she had found the aircraft. At 3 the following morning the observer, Sub-Lieutenant (A) R. G. Drake, R.N., signalled that all the crew had

END OF A GERMAN SUPPLY SHIP. Reconnaissance aircraft from the Eagle pierced the neutral disguise of this German supply ship in the South Atlantic in June, 1941. *Above*, she is seen on fire through the struts of one of the Swordfish that bombed her.

DIRECT HIT. *Above*, she is struck by a bomb amidships, while two more drop in the water beside her. *Below*, her crew abandon her, as she settles by the stern.

been rescued alive and were on board, bound for Teneriffe.

When the Cabo de Buena Esperanza reached Teneriffe the arrival of the naval airmen raised a knotty problem of international law. They had been picked up outside territorial waters, but Teneriffe is a Spanish possession. Were the crew to be interned, or not? After what the Vice-Admiral Commanding the North Altantic Station described as "considerable telegraphing," the Spanish authorities decided to solve the question by releasing the crew and interning the Swordfish.

German shipping was frequently found to be sailing under neutral flags. In June, 1941, when the Eagle was operating in the South Atlantic, one of her aircraft on anti-submarine patrol reported the Norwegian steamer Kristiania Fjord 30 miles from the carrier. On being sighted she altered course and increased speed. It seemed evident that the vessel was disguised, and an armed searching force was despatched to make her close the Eagle for examination. If she failed to comply, she was to be attacked with bombs.

One of the searching aircraft sighted her after 90 minutes' flying and signalled her to alter course. She paid no attention. The aircraft opened fire across her bows with the rear gun, but she continued to steam at full speed. The aircraft dropped two 500-lb. bombs, which fell 20 feet from the port side amidships, then shadowed her for a further two hours. The pilot eventually landed back on the Eagle with barely ten minutes' petrol left, having been in the air for over five hours.

Meanwhile another striking force had been despatched, led by Lieutenant-Commander A. J. Debenham, D.S.C., R.N. They found the ship stopped, on fire, and being abandoned. The Norwegian ensign had been hauled down. Two boats were lying off and another was being manned under the stern. Lieutenant-Commander Debenham ordered the ship to steer to the southward. There was no response to his signal. The striking force then attacked the ship with bombs, obtaining

one direct hit abaft the funnel and three near misses. They left her settling by the stern and blazing fiercely. She sent out an S.O.S. in German to all ships stating that she was being bombed by aircraft and had scuttled herself, revealing her identity as the Elbe. At daylight next morning the Eagle's aircraft searched for the boats to a depth of 60 miles, sighting nothing but oil, wreckage and a large number of empty 50-gallon drums, which suggested that the Elbe had been a submarine supply ship.

Some weeks later the Eagle's Swordfish intercepted a similar enemy vessel flying the Dutch flag. When ordered to stop, the crew began to take to the boats, but were compelled to return to the ship by machine-gun fire, which was directed on the water. To prevent the ship being scuttled the aircraft remained over her for nearly five hours until H.M.S. Dunedin came up and put a prize crew aboard. The vessel was found to be carrying a large stock of torpedoes and other stores, together with reliefs for the submarine crews.

No reconnaissance by naval aircraft has made a greater contribution to the success of momentous operations than that which brought the news that the German battleship Bismarck and the heavy cruiser Prinz Eugen had sailed from Bergen.

The two ships left Kiel on 19th May, 1941, and were sighted and photographed on the 21st in one of the unfrequented fiords near Bergen by an aircraft of Coastal Command. In the afternoon the weather broke and became so bad that a further reconnaissance across the North Sea was perilous. Next morning flying conditions were even worse. Nevertheless it was of vital importance to the Commander-in-Chief, Home Fleet, to know whether the ships were still in the fiord or whether they had put to sea, for until he had that information it was impossible for him to dispose his forces to the best advantage.

Captain H. L. St. J. Fancourt, R.N., who was then in command of the naval air station in the Orkneys (H.M.S. Sparrowhawk), accordingly obtained permission to send out a reconnaissance aircraft in an attempt to break through the fog belt on the Norwegian coast. Commander G. A. Rotherham, O.B.E., R.N., an observer of great experience, but as executive officer of the station not appointed for flying duties, volunteered to go, and Lieutenant (A) N. E. Goddard, R.N.V.R., volunteered to act as his pilot. They were accompanied by Leading Airmen Milne and Armstrong. The aircraft selected was an American-built Glenn-Martin Maryland, attached to the station for target-towing.

Shortly after the Maryland had flown off, the R.A.F. reported that weather conditions were impossible for reconnaissance on the Norwegian coast. The situation was so grave, however, that Captain Fancourt felt justified in not recalling the aircraft.

The R.A.F. reports had been no exaggeration. The weather was so thick that the pilot was compelled to fly at almost surface level, and more than once came down to within 50 feet without being able to see the water. As he approached the Norwegian coast, however, he found a small break in the mist. The observer's navigation proved accurate and at a height of 1,500 feet the Maryland swept round the fiord where the German warships had been seen and photographed. The fiord was empty. Not content with this, Commander Rotherham took the aircraft low over Bergen harbour, encountering intense anti-aircraft fire. There was still no sign of either the Bismarck or the Prinz Eugen. He reported that the enemy had put to sea and then navigated the Maryland back to the Shetlands.

The qualifications of the crew were such that the Commander-in-Chief had no hesitation in accepting the report, and it was on the information provided by this intelligence that the Home Fleet put to sea in pursuit of the Bismarck and Prinz Eugen. Both observer and pilot were decorated for their skilful and determined reconnaissance.

7. SPOTTING FOR THE FLEET

CLOSELY connected with naval aircraft's function of reconnaissance is that of spotting for the gunfire of the Fleet, both on sea and land targets, a highly skilled duty of first importance, particularly in long-range actions.

The first occasion on which an aircraft was thus employed in the present war was during the Battle of the River Plate. After the Admiral Graf Spee's encounter with S.S. Doric Star in the neighbourhood of St. Helena on 3rd December, 1939, Commodore (now Admiral Sir) H. H. Harwood, commanding the South American Division, and flying his broad pendant in H.M.S. Ajax, correctly anticipated that the raider would cross the South Atlantic, and estimated that she would reach the area of the River Plate by the morning of 13th December. He had with him two other cruisers, the Achilles, detached from the New Zealand Division and manned mainly by New Zealanders, and the Exeter. H.M.S. Cumberland, the largest and most powerful of his force, was refitting in the Falkland Islands.

At dawn on 13th December the enemy was sighted. She opened fire with her main armament at a range of nearly ten miles. The three cruisers replied, rapidly closing the range. The Ajax carried two Seafox floatplanes, one of which had been fuelled ready for action. When the Graf Spee was sighted the pilot, Lieutenant E. D. G. Lewin, R.N., gave orders for the aircraft and catapult to be cleared away. By the time he and his observer, Lieutenant R. E. N. Kearney,

R.N., had taken their places the Ajax was under fire and they were subjected to severe blast from the guns of her two after turrets, which were replying on a forward bearing. The aircraft was whipping badly and the second Seafox was damaged by blast. It was therefore essential to launch the aircraft as soon as possible and it was catapulted off at 6.37. The Exeter's two Walruses were both hit by splinters before they could be flown off, and consequently the responsibility for spotting the Force's gunfire devolved upon the single Seafox.

The morning was fine and clear, with extreme visibility. Lieutenant Lewin took up his position on the disengaged bow of the Ajax, climbing to the cloud base at 3,000 feet, so that he could take refuge in the clouds if attacked by the Graf Spee's aircraft : he did not then know that it had been put out of action by gunfire. The Seafox had been only a minute in the air when the Exeter received two more hits from the Graf Spee's 11-inch shells. She completely disappeared in smoke and flame and the watchers in the sky thought she had gone. But she emerged and continued to fire her guns, although she was forced to fall out of the action later.

Soon the engagement became a chase, the Ajax and Achilles making 31 knots as the Graf Spee frequently altered course and used smoke screens in an attempt to escape further punishment. The Seafox spotted for both cruisers and enabled them to make rapid and accurate fire, although the smoke and flashes from the enemy's guns made the observer's task very difficult. The Graf Spee was fighting obstinately and by 7.30 had put

"SPEE HAS BLOWN HERSELF UP." The ruined Graf Spee blazes outside Montevideo on 17th December, 1939. Throughout the action of 13th December a Seafox from the Ajax spotted for the British cruisers' gunfire. This Seafox watched the Graf Spee every day in harbour, and finally gave the waiting cruisers the news " Spee has blown herself up."

four of the Ajax's guns out of action. She was taking severe punishment herself, however, and Lieutenant Lewin closed her in an attempt to discover the extent of the damage. The Graf Spee opened on him with her anti-aircraft guns, holing both the starboard main planes, and since the aircraft's primary duty was to spot for the cruisers' fire-control he retired out of range. By counting the fall of shell, he judged that the enemy had received at least 30 hits ; this proved to be an under-estimate.

A few minutes later the observer saw the Graf Spee fire several torpedoes at a range of about five miles. He signalled, " Torpedoes approaching. They will pass ahead of you." The Commodore decided to take no chances, and altered course towards the enemy. By 7.38 he had reduced the range to four miles and the Seafox's report showed the cruisers' fire to be deadly. Owing to the danger of ammunition shortage, however, the Commodore decided to break off the action and to shadow the enemy until nightfall, when he would have a better chance of closing to a range at which he could use his lighter armament and his torpedoes decisively.

The Seafox was then ordered to find the Exeter and tell her to close the Commodore. She was 18 miles astern, and in no condition to fight another action. The Seafox passed the cruisers' position, course and speed to her, and then returned. There was a high sea running, but Lieutenant Lewin made a successful landing alongside and the aircraft was recovered skilfully and—equally important—without loss of time. It was then refuelled and prepared for another flight.

The Graf Spee made continued but un-availing attempts to shake off the two cruisers and shortly after midnight sought refuge in Montevideo. While she remained there the Seafox made a daily reconnais-sance, the pilot taking care not to fly over territorial waters. About 5.30 p.m. on 17th December the Commodore learnt that she had weighed anchor. He took the Ajax

and Achilles, in company with the Cumber-land (which had reached the scene of action from the southward in 34 hours), towards the entrance of the channel leading to the Roads. The Seafox took up a position on the starboard bow of the Ajax, ready to spot for the second battle that appeared imminent.

When the enemy failed to appear the Seafox was ordered to report her movements and those of the German merchant ship Tacoma, to which she was known to have transferred 700 of her men. The Graf Spee was observed to be lying in shallow water about six miles to the south-west of Monte-video. Lieutenant Lewin closed her as near as he could without entering territorial waters. One small craft was seen on her way from the Graf Spee to a merchant ship hove-to in the Channel.

A few minutes before sunset there were two large explosions from fore and aft of the Graf Spee, followed by a third amidships. At first Lieutenant Lewin thought she was firing her main armament. But by that time there was no one left aboard the Graf Spee. The explosions were caused by the delayed-action fuses set by the demolition party, which had withdrawn to the merchant ship. At 8.54 the Seafox signalled, " Spee has blown herself up."

By that time it was too dark to identify the Tacoma without entering territorial waters, but there was no doubt that she was the merchant ship lying in the channel. The Seafox returned to the flagship, which was steaming towards Montevideo. As she was recovering her aircraft the Achilles passed her, and both companies cheered ship.

" It was now dark," wrote Rear-Admiral Harwood (who had received his promotion immediately the results of the battle became known in London), " and she was ablaze from end to end, flames reaching almost as high as the top of the control tower, a magnificent and most cheering sight."

Lieutenant Lewin received the D.S.C. for

his part in the action ; Lieutenant Kearney was mentioned in despatches. These were the first honours gained by the Fleet Air Arm during the present war.

Spotting for the Fleet during a bombardment is a duty no less important than spotting at sea, and the assistance of the aircraft enables the ships to use indirect fire with great advantage. The closest co-operation is necessary between the crew of the spotting aircraft and the ship's Gunnery Officer and W/T. staff, and the work also demands efficient teamwork between pilot and observer. It is a duty which puts the crew of the spotting aircraft to the severest test. They have none of the excitement that the T.B.R. or fighter airmen know. Their duty is to watch, not to attack. They are in peril from anti-aircraft guns and enemy fighters, and the pilot must keep accurate station and give his observer all the help he can in the difficult task of marking and reporting the fall of the shells in the din and smoke of battle.

An example of spotting carried out in the most exacting conditions was when H.M.S. Galatea bombarded enemy positions near Calais in May, 1940. Two spotting aircraft were used, and although neither the ship nor the aircraft knew the exact position of the targets, indirect fire was completely successful.

At the dawn bombardment of Genoa by Force H in February, 1941, on the other hand, preliminary co-operation between the ships and the aircraft was possible and produced excellent results. The observers rehearsed the whole operation in every detail and practised on a plaster model of the objective for days beforehand. After an initial landfall well south of Genoa, the ships did not see the land again owing to the low visibility and depended entirely on the spotting aircraft for the accuracy of fire control. Spotting was carried out by catapult aircraft from the ships of Force H, the Ark Royal sending three Swordfish, with an escort of Fulmars, as stand-by spotters.

Naval aircraft have also spotted during many sea bombardments of coastal targets in the Western Desert, although at times the observers have had great difficulty in picking up the few landmarks available, and the clouds of sand raised by the fall of shells soon tend to obscure the target area.

During night bombardments the spotting aircraft drop flares to illuminate the targets. In April, 1941, when the Fleet bombarded Tripoli, each firing ship had one spotter and one flare-dropper, and in spite of the dust that had been thrown up by a previous bombing attack, the results were satisfactory.

When necessary, fighter escort has been provided. During the naval bombardment of Bardia in August, 1940, the Eagle's Gladiators, co-operating with the shore-based aircraft of the R.A.A.F., provided effective cover for the spotting Swordfish and the Fleet. If a spotter is driven off by enemy fighters, as happened during the bombardment of Calais, the stand-by aircraft takes over its duty.

There have been occasions when catapult aircraft, besides spotting for the Fleet, have taken an offensive part in the action. When H.M.S. Dorsetshire bombarded the port of Dante, in Italian Somaliland, on 18th November, 1940, her Walrus was flown off armed with bombs. While dropping the bombs on a fuel tank ashore, a difficult target at the bottom of a *nullah*, the crew engaged in a machine-gun duel with one of the covering batteries. Several bullets hit the aircraft and the port petrol tank was put out of action. They then tried to locate the position of a 5·8 battery, and were able to report that it did not exist.

After this preliminary work, the Dorsetshire hoisted her battle ensign and opened fire on a large loading-stage in the harbour. It was soon ablaze and the cruiser then shifted her fire to two storage houses.

Thanks to the efficient spotting of the Walrus these were soon destroyed. " Cease Fire " was then ordered and the Walrus was hoisted in and re-armed with bombs.

Although the damage to the port petrol tank had reduced the aircraft's performance by half, the crew begged to be allowed to make a second flight and an hour later bombed another tank ashore.

The bombardment of Dante shows that catapult aircraft need not necessarily be restricted to spotting or reconnaissance in a naval action, and during the Second Battle of Narvik H.M.S. Warspite's aircraft, a Swordfish fitted with floats, acted as a kind of aerial maid-of-all-work to the Fleet.

On the morning of 13th April, 1940, the Warspite, wearing the flag of Vice-Admiral Sir W. J. Whitworth, K.C.B., D.S.O., and screened by nine destroyers, passed through the entrance to Ofot Fiord, leading to Narvik, which lay some 30 miles ahead. At 11.52, when five miles west of Baroy Island, the Warspite catapulted her aircraft with orders to reconnoitre ahead of the Force as it advanced up the fiord, and to bomb any suitable targets. The observer was Lieutenant-Commander W. L. M. Brown, R.N., the pilot, Petty Officer F. C. Rice, with Leading Airman M. G. Pacey as the air-gunner.

Low clouds formed a ceiling between the steep cliffs, and as the Swordfish proceeded up the fiord it was like flying in a tunnel. The first ship to be sighted was a German destroyer steering to the westward. The British destroyers in the van opened fire and she retired at long range. Meanwhile Petty Officer Rice observed a submarine at anchor 50 yards from the jetty at Bjerkvik. The Swordfish dived to 300 feet to release its bombs. The first hit the bows of the submarine. Owing to the explosion the second bomb's exact point of impact was difficult to observe, but it was either a hit or a near miss. The air-gunner raked the conning tower with a burst from the rear gun. The submarine sank within half a minute, but had had time to open fire, and damaged the tail plane of the Swordfish, making it sluggish on the controls so that the pilot had to manœuvre gently during the rest of the flight.

At 12.40 Lieutenant-Commander Brown reported that an enemy destroyer was hiding in a bay five miles ahead of the screen (presumably hoping to remain unseen against the rocky background) in a position to fire torpedoes at the advancing Force. The leading destroyers turned their guns and torpedo armament on the starboard bow, and before the enemy could fire more than one salvo he was heavily engaged. One torpedo from the Bedouin and another from the Eskimo struck her, and in three minutes she was on fire fore and aft. Salvoes from the Warspite's guns completed her

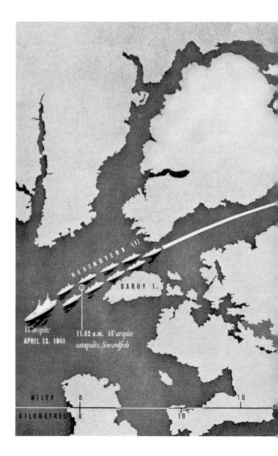

DESTROYERS (I)

BAROY I.

Warspite
APRIL 13. 1940

11.52 a.m. Warspite
catapults Swordfish

MILES   0   10
KILOMETRES 0   10

destruction. Shortly after this action Lieutenant-Commander Brown sighted five torpedo tracks approaching the Force and gave timely warning. They passed clear and exploded against the cliffs of the fiord.

Narvik lies near the entrance to Rombaks Fiord, into which three enemy destroyers were seen to retire under the cover of smoke screens. Five of the British destroyers pursued them, while others entered Narvik harbour and attacked another German destroyer, which caught fire under the combined attack and blew up later. All resistance in the harbour then ceased.

The Swordfish proceeded to reconnoitre the position in Rombaks Fiord. The Warspite was engaging the enemy, and the smoke from her exploding shells, combined with the low clouds and the steepness of the cliffs on either side of the narrow fiord, made observation and visual signalling very difficult. At 3 p.m., however, the Swordfish reported two enemy destroyers at the head of the fiord. The Eskimo engaged them, closely followed by the Forester and the Hero. The enemy replied with gunfire and torpedoes, and the Eskimo had her bow blown away. Then one of the German destroyers ran aground. The

THE SECOND BATTLE OF NARVIK, 13th APRIL, 1940. *The numbers in brackets on the map refer to photographs on the following page*

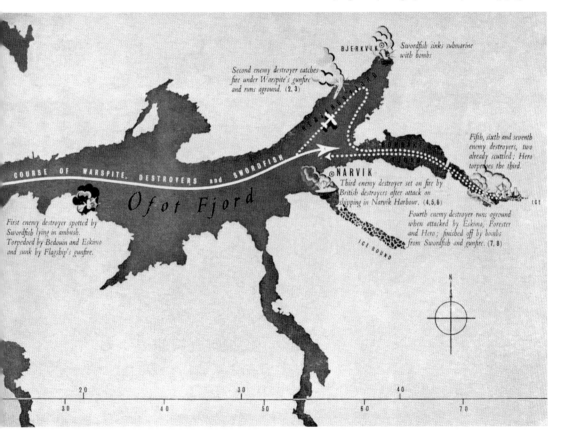

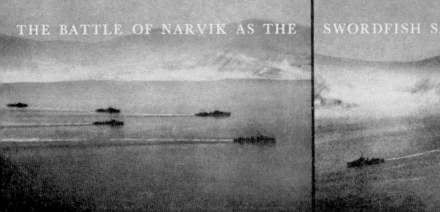

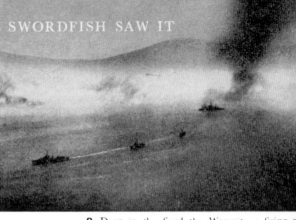

1. The British destroyer force, screening the Warspite, enters Ofot Fiord. This and most of the following pictures were taken from the Flagship's Swordfish.

2. Deep in the fiord the Warspite is firing at a German destroyer. Three of the British destroyers can be seen in the foreground

4. This destroyer was sheltering in Narvik Bay. She was attacked by the British destroyers, and is here seen drifting into Ofot Fiord.

5. Her guns silenced, and burning furiously, the destroyer drifted all through the night lighting up the fiord. In the morning she sank

7. The Eskimo, in ripple-circle, is hit by a torpedo from the distant enemy destroyer. Note the shell-tear in the Swordfish tail plane. The Hero stands by in foreground

8. In the inner recesses of Rombaks Fiord the remaining four enemy destroyers were trapped. Here one of them is aground. She was later bombed by the Swordfish

3. Beached against the snow-covered rocks of Herjangs Fiord, the same destroyer burns herself out. Swordfish struts are outlined in foreground

6. All resistance ceased in Narvik Harbour where the shore batteries were silenced and an enemy transport lay wrecked and aground

9. With the entire force of seven German destroyers wiped out, the Warspite and destroyer screen steam out through the narrow exit of Ofot Fiord.

Swordfish dropped its remaining bombs on her and she was finished off by gunfire. The other destroyer retired under the cover of smoke to the top of the fiord.

At 3.30 the Bedouin signalled that both she and the Hero had almost exhausted their ammunition and that the remaining three enemy destroyers were lurking round a corner of the inner fiord, out of sight, and in a position of great advantage if they still had torpedoes. Vice-Admiral Whitworth replied :

" The torpedo menace must be accepted. Enemy must be destroyed without delay. Take Kimberley, Forester, Hero and Punjabi under your orders and organize attack, sending most serviceable destroyer first. Ram or board if necessary."

When the destroyers proceeded up the fiord, however, there was no reply to their fire. The enemy had abandoned the three vessels. One had been scuttled, another was sinking, and the third was sent to the bottom by a torpedo from the Hero. This ended the main action, and the Swordfish returned to the Warspite, having been four hours in the air. During that time it had passed back vital information about the position of the enemy ships, besides reporting torpedo tracks, taking photographs, bombing a destroyer and sinking a submarine.

The total German naval forces present had been sunk without the loss of a British ship, for both the Eskimo and the Cossack (which had drifted on to a submerged wreck in Narvik Bay) were able to return with the Force.

" The cumulative effect of the roar of Warspite's 15-inch guns reverberating down and around the high mountains of the fiord, the bursts and splashes of these great shells, the sight of their ships sinking and burning around them, must have been terrifying to the enemy," wrote the Vice-Admiral in his official despatch. " The enemy reports made by Warspite's aircraft were invaluable," he added. " I doubt if ever a ship-borne aircraft has been used to such good purpose as it was in this operation."

STRIKING FORCE

THE TORPEDO AIRCRAFT

8. THE TRIUMPH AT TARANTO

In the second battle of Narvik the Warspite's Swordfish performed all the functions of a T.B.R. aircraft except that of torpedo dropping. In that action, fought at close range against small ships, in restricted waters, the torpedo could be used with better effect by the destroyers, but against capital ships it remains the most powerful and flexible weapon of air warfare, in fact the only one with which aircraft have a reasonable chance of inflicting vital damage on a battleship, since it can open her up below the water-line. The proportion of hits increases with the number of aircraft engaged.

The possibility of releasing torpedoes from aircraft was first demonstrated in 1911, when an Italian, Captain Guidoni, dropped a 352-lb. torpedo from an 80 h.p. Farman aircraft. In the same year certain British naval officers, among them Commodore (now Rear-Admiral Sir) Murray Sueter and Lieutenant D. H. Hyde-Thomson, R.N., began to interest themselves in the torpedo as an aerial weapon, and as a result of their experiments Mr. Thomas Sopwith was invited to build a special torpedo-carrying aircraft. Towards the end of 1913 the first flight with a 14-inch torpedo was carried out at Calshot in a 200 h.p. Sopwith Canton-Unné seaplane. The experiments were continued, and H.M.S. Engadine, the converted cross-channel steamer, was specially fitted to carry three 160 h.p. Short Gnome torpedo-seaplanes.

The first successful use of torpedo-aircraft was in August, 1915, when Flight-Commander C. H. K. Edmonds, R.N., operating from the former Isle of Man packet Ben-my-Chree in a Short 184 seaplane, sank a Turkish merchant vessel of 5,000 tons in the Dardanelles with a 14-inch torpedo.

After the war a Torpedo Development Flight was started at Gosport under R.A.F. control with a Lieutenant-Commander ap-pointed to naval liaison duties. The torpedo used was the 18-inch, Mark VIII, which had been made for use by submarines. Although this weapon has been improved, the principles of its use remain unchanged. To run properly, a torpedo must enter the water at an angle approximate to the direction of its flight, that is to say like an arrow flying through the air. If it enters the water too steeply it will dive, if it is dropped flat the result is a " belly-flop ", which will damage the intricate mechanism. Before the war it was considered that the aircraft should be in level flight on release, but recent experience has enabled the pilot to drop his torpedo at a greater height and when travelling faster than formerly. The torpedo now in use is an improved variety of the 18-inch, weighing 1,500 lb.

During a daylight attack clouds will give protection to a striking force during its approach, but may increase the difficulty of attaining a good position for the strike. In night attacks, so long as information is sufficiently accurate to ensure contact being made, flares may be dropped to illuminate the target, but will eliminate the possibility of surprise. Moonlight gives a better chance of success, since the ship may be visible for several miles. The most suitable time for a torpedo attack, however, is at dawn, for then the aircraft can observe the ships but remain invisible until the moment of the strike. Dusk is less suitable, since the striking force is less likely to make its approach unseen and must return to the carrier in darkness.

Successful torpedo attacks can be expected only from highly-trained pilots, who require constant practice even after they have joined a carrier-borne squadron. It would be idle to pretend that every torpedo strike delivered by naval aircraft in this war has been successful. Success, in war as in peace, is the result of previous failure, and from every abortive attack valuable experience has been gained.

Failure was the result of the first torpedo attack in history against a screened capital ship at sea : the German battle-cruiser Scharnhorst. She had already been dive-bombed by a striking force of 15 Skuas from the Ark Royal while lying at anchor off Trondheim on 13th June, 1940, but although the Skuas had pressed home their attack with great gallantry the results had been indecisive and eight failed to return. On 21st June, a Sunderland flying-boat sighted the Scharnhorst steaming at high speed to the southward, escorted by seven destroyers. While the Sunderland shadowed her, six Swordfish—all that were available at the time—were despatched from the Orkneys to attack her with torpedoes. They made contact with her after flying for 240 miles, and both sub-flights dived to the attack. Unfortunately, their approach had been observed and they met with intense anti-aircraft fire from the Scharnhorst and the screen. Two Swordfish were shot down and no hits were scored.

Even more disappointing to the striking force concerned was the unsuccessful attack on the Tirpitz by twelve Albacores from H.M.S. Victorious. At 8.42 a.m. on 9th March, 1942, the striking force sighted the Tirpitz steaming in the direction of Narvik, escorted by only one destroyer, at a distance of 20 miles. The leader's intention was to take his squadron through the cloud until he was ahead of the ship, but shortly before he passed over her a break in the cloud revealed his position at a critical moment, forcing him to attack from a disadvantageous tactical position, so that the Tirpitz had time to comb the torpedo tracks. No reduction of speed or other signs of damage were observed, but two Albacores were shot down.

None realized the gravity of this failure more bitterly than the crews themselves. As the Commanding Officer of the Victorious said : " It was a chance they had dreamed and prayed for," and, as they knew only too well, it was a chance that might not come again.

The Fleet Air Arm can afford to be frank about its failures, since its achievements have been high, and these events have been described to show the intricacy of the pilots' task even when conditions are favourable for a torpedo attack : and often they are far from favourable. A torpedo is the key which will open up the armour of a battle-ship, but the ability to use it rightly depends upon the skill of the user, upon the boldness of the attack, upon careful reconnaissance, and—not least—upon a striking force large enough to ensure the requisite number of hits.

The first successful torpedo attack on a capital ship from the air was when 12 Swordfish from the Ark Royal, flying in three waves, torpedoed and immobilized the French battle-cruiser Dunkerque at Mers-el-Kebir (Oran) on 6th July, 1940, but the outstanding achievement came on 11th November with the attack on the Italian fleet at Taranto.

This attack had been long prepared. In peace time navies must plan for war, and in 1938, when war appeared inevitable, Admiral (now Admiral of the Fleet) Sir A. Dudley P. R. Pound, K.C.B., G.C.V.O., Commander-in-Chief of the Mediterranean Fleet, requested Captain (now Vice-Admiral Sir) A. L. St. G. Lyster, C.V.O., D.S.O., commanding the Glorious, to draw up plans for attacking the Italian fleet in Taranto harbour with his T.B.R. squadrons, which were very highly trained, particularly in night flying.

After Italy entered the war her main fleet, consisting of six battleships—two of the new Littorio class and four of the recently reconstructed Cavour and Duilio class—about five cruisers, and twenty destroyers, was based on Taranto. These ships emerged only to return at high speed in time to prevent Admiral Cunningham from coming to grips with them. Rear-Admiral Lyster,

SNAKE'S COIL. The Tirpitz twists and turns as she detects the force of Albacores from the Victorious about to attack her. The German battleship was steaming towards Narvik on 9th March, 1942. This photograph from one of the Albacores was taken looking down through the cloudbreak that, too soon revealed their position.

then commanding Mediterranean Aircraft Carriers and flying his flag in the Illustrious, wrote to the Commander-in-Chief, " They show no inclination to venture far from the Gulf of Taranto, and since it is not easy to find any inducement to make them do so, air attack in the harbour must be considered."

There were several requirements to ensure reasonable prospects of success. The most important was timely photographic reconnaissance, to show not only that the battleships were in harbour but where they were berthed. An undetected approach to the flying-off position was also essential and this involved fitting the aircraft with long-range petrol tanks. The pilots and observers needed special night-flying training before they could make the long and hazardous flight, and it was not until mid-October

that they were ready. The majority of the air crews who had practised the original plans in the Glorious were then in the Illustrious.

The attack was to have taken place on 21st October—Trafalgar Day—but was postponed until 11th November, while the Mediterranean Fleet was covering important warship reinforcements and convoy movements. It was intended that the Eagle should combine with the Illustrious in the operation, but two days before the Fleet was due to sail from Alexandria she developed serious defects to her petrol system (caused by many near misses from Italian dive-bombers) and had to be left behind. She embarked five of her Swordfish, with eight pilots and eight observers, in the Illustrious.

On the morning of the 11th an aircraft was flown to Malta to collect the photographs of Taranto harbour which R.A.F. aircraft from Malta had taken on the previous day. They showed that the Italian fleet—including five battleships—was still in harbour and contributed much to the success of the attack. The R.A.F. also patrolled the Gulf of Taranto until 10.30 that evening, and was able to report that a sixth battleship had entered the harbour.

At 6 p.m., when the Mediterranean Fleet was to the westward of the Island of Zante, the Commander-in-Chief detached the Illustrious (Captain, now Rear-Admiral, D. W. Boyd, C.B.E., D.S.C.) with an escort of four cruisers and four destroyers. On reaching the flying-off position the first striking force of 12 Swordfish was ranged on the flight-deck, led by Lieutenant-Commander K. Williamson, R.N., with Lieutenant N. J. Scarlett, R.N., as his observer. The reconnaissance photographs showed the harbour to be protected by balloons and nets, which made suitable torpedo-dropping positions restricted, therefore only six aircraft were armed with torpedoes ; four carried bombs and two carried bombs and flares. The torpedo-carriers were to attack the battleships lying in the outer harbour (the Mar Grande) and, as a diversion, the bombers were to deliver a synchronised attack on the cruisers and destroyers alongside the quay and in the inner harbour (the Mar Piccolo). No air-gunners were taken, to enable the aircraft to carry internal auxiliary tanks.

The striking force formed up eight miles from the Illustrious and at 8.57 set course for Taranto, distant 170 miles. Flying conditions were good. The moon was three-quarters full. There was thin cloud at 8,000 feet. At 9.15 the squadron became separated in cloud and had to continue with five torpedo-aircraft, one bomber and two flare-droppers, leaving the four remaining aircraft to attack independently. At 10.56 the flare-droppers were detached and the first laid a line of flares along the eastern side of the harbour. This aircraft, with the stand-by flare-dropper, then made a dive-bombing attack on an oil-storage depot and set it on fire.

As the flares lit up the harbour the first sub-flight went in to the attack at 4,000 feet over San Pietro Island, led by Lieutenant-Commander Williamson, who was last seen over the centre of the Mar Grande. The second aircraft of the sub-flight came down to within 30 feet of the water half way across the harbour and attacked one of the Cavour class battleships at a range of 700 yards. There was an explosion in the ship a minute later. The pilot made a sharp turn to port over the Taranto shoal breakwater, meeting intense flak from the batteries at the entrance to the harbour. The remaining pilot of the sub-flight attacked the same target. Those who followed him selected the two Littorio class battleships and reported hits. One saw a column of smoke rising abaft the funnels. By that time the cruisers had opened fire and were hitting the merchant ships in the harbour. Three of the barrage balloons were set alight as a result of the anti-aircraft fire. For some reason the Italians used no searchlights. The balloon barrage did not impede the pilots unduly. One sang out to his observer, " Where's that bloody balloon barrage ? " " We've been through it once," was the answer, " and we're just going through it again."

Captain Oliver Patch, R.M., who was in one of the bombing aircraft, had some difficulty in identifying his target, but finally dive-bombed two cruisers from 1,500 feet. Another of the bombers dropped a stick across four of the destroyers, and a third, who could not find the target in the Mar Piccolo, continued along the southern shore and attacked the seaplane base, scoring a direct hit on the hangar. One of the observers was afraid that his bombs had failed to drop. To make sure, the pilot climbed up again, dived a second time through the barrage, and repeated the attack. In spite of the intense anti-aircraft fire during and after the attack, Lieutenant-Commander Williamson's aircraft was the only one which failed to return to the ship.

Meanwhile the second striking force of nine Swordfish, led by Lieutenant-Commander J. W. Hale, R.N., with Lieutenant G. A. Carline, R.N., as his observer, began flying off at 9.23 p.m. Five were armed with torpedoes, two with bombs, and two with flares and bombs. While taxi-ing forward, the eighth Swordfish, piloted by Lieutenant E. W. Clifford, R.N., collided with the last of the range and had to be struck down for repairs. The observer, Lieutenant G. R. M. Going, R.N., while on patrol in a Swordfish that morning, had forced-landed in the sea 20 miles from the carrier. He and the telegraphist-air-gunner had been shot over the nose, head first into the water (" a most comfortable way to ditch," as he remarked, " no pain being suffered by anyone ") and had been picked up by H.M.S. Gloucester and flown back in her Walrus to the Illustrious.

While Clifford was urging the maintenance ratings to get the Swordfish fit to fly, Going begged the Captain's leave to follow the striking force, saying that he thought they would be able to reach Taranto in time for the attack. They were allowed to go, and took off 20 minutes after the others.

After the striking force had been flying for 20 minutes a defect forced one of the Swordfish to return to the carrier. The remainder sighted the flares and flak while they were still 60 miles from Taranto. Just before midnight, the flare-droppers were detached and the torpedo aircraft attacked the battleships. One pilot, while diving to the attack, had his aircraft knocked out of control by machine-gun bullets hitting the outer aileron rod. He regained control a moment later. As he came down to the water level he could see one of the Littorio class battleships silhouetted against the flares and the moon, and dropped his torpedo on her port quarter, his port wing being hit as he made his getaway.

The cruisers, the shore batteries and the battleships were firing now. The battleships seemed to be hitting the cruisers, and the cruisers hit several of the merchant ships in

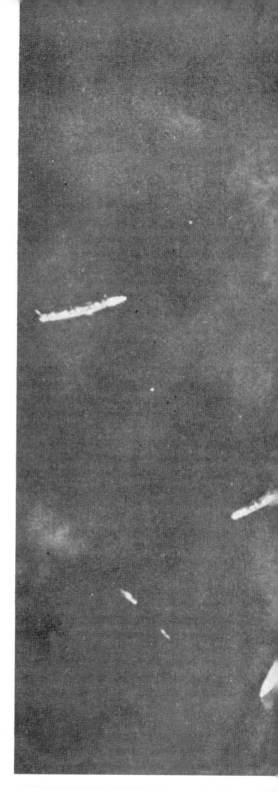

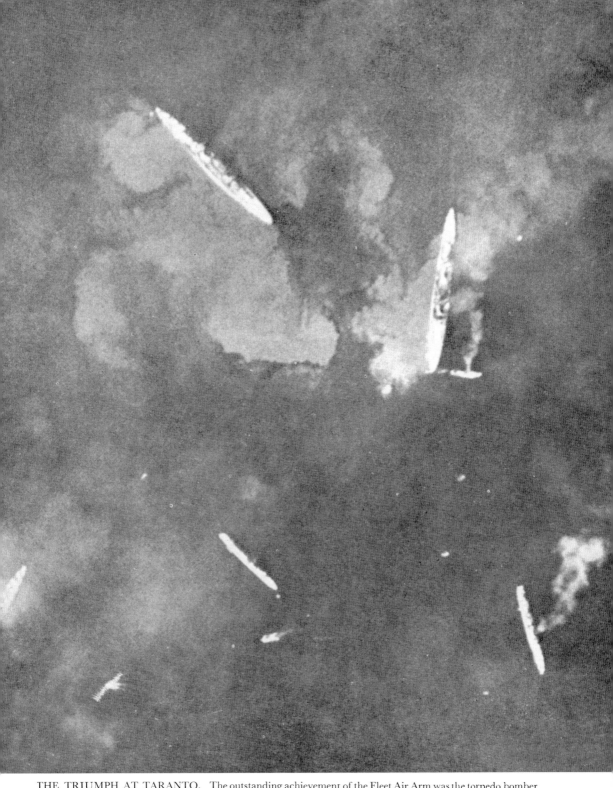

THE TRIUMPH AT TARANTO. The outstanding achievement of the Fleet Air Arm was the torpedo bomber attack on the Italian naval base of Taranto on the night of 11th November, 1940. The picture shows, towards the top, two cruisers of the Bolzano and Trento classes, badly damaged and surrounded by oil, in the inner harbour. The other ships are four destroyers and a second Trento class cruiser. In another part of the harbour three of Italy's six battleships were severely damaged.

the harbour and set them ablaze. The Swordfish had to fly through this criss-cross of fire. The air stank with incendiary bullets. Flaming onions seemed to go floating past and burn out. One observer had a vivid impression of a circle of stabbing flame. He wondered how they were going to get out of it. As the pilot dropped his torpedo he came down so low that his undercarriage touched the surface, sending up an enormous column of water behind, but they succeeded in pulling out.

By the time the aircraft piloted by Lieutenant Clifford reached the scene the main attack had been delivered some 15 minutes previously. The whole harbour was lit up with burning ships, and the Italian gunners concentrated their fire on the single Swordfish as it dived through the barrage to drop its bombs across the line of cruisers.

One Swordfish failed to return. It was last seen following the Squadron Commander in to the attack. The remainder had landed on the carrier by 2.30 a.m., and the Force rejoined the Commander-in-Chief. To those engaged it seemed miraculous that the losses were no heavier. " Only Swordfish ", said one of them, " with their manœuvrability and their capacity for turning and twisting, could have got through that fire."

Later, in Greece, this officer was interrogating an Italian pilot who had been shot down in Greece. When questioned about Taranto, where he had been stationed at the time of the attack, he expressed the utmost admiration for the British air crews. He could not understand, he said, how they had come through that fire. When the interrogating officer mentioned that he had been one of them, a broad grin of admiration spread across the Italian's face and he shook him warmly by both hands.

The results of the attack were not known for certain until two days later, when a photographic reconnaissance by the R.A.F. showed the Littorio lying with a heavy list and her fo'c'sle awash, one Cavour class battleship with her stern under water as far as the after turret, and one Duilio class beached and abandoned. There was no direct evidence as to the damage suffered by the cruisers, but two were seen listing to starboard surrounded by oil fuel. Two fleet auxiliaries were lying with their sterns under water ; the seaplane base and the oil storage depot had been damaged.

A second attack had been planned for the night of 12th November, and a striking force of 15 aircraft was prepared, but owing to the unfavourable weather report the operation was cancelled.

Writing of the zeal and enthusiasm of all who took part in this great enterprise, Captain Boyd declared : " It is impossible to praise too highly those who in these comparatively slow machines made studied and accurate attacks in the midst of intense anti-aircraft fire. It is hoped that this victory will be considered a suitable reward to those whose work and faith in the Fleet Air Arm has made it possible."

" England needs a victory," said Sir John Jervis before the Battle of St. Vincent. She needed one before the Battle of Taranto, and the Fleet Air Arm gave her one when she was despondent after many months of defeat. Half the Italian battle fleet had been put out of action for the loss of two aircraft, one officer killed and three taken prisoners. The victory vastly increased Admiral Cunningham's freedom of action in the Mediterranean and enabled him to release two battleships for operations elsewhere. As an example of economy of force, the engagement was unsurpassed.

Credit is also due to the fighters of the Illustrious. In spite of the enemy's determined attempt to find the Fleet during these operations only three erratic attacks were made on Admiral Cunningham's widely dispersed forces, and the Fulmars shot down eight Italian aircraft without loss to themselves. As a result of this mauling the Regia Aeronautica made no serious attempt to interfere with the Mediterranean Fleet until the arrival of the Luftwaffe in January, 1941.

9. FIND, FIX AND STRIKE

THE destruction of the Italian battleships at Taranto was the logical outcome of the attack on the Dunkerque at Oran, which had shown that torpedo aircraft could strike effectively at a capital ship in harbour, and for the first time in history the Navy had won a battle without firing a gun ; but the Fleet Air Arm still awaited its opportunity to prove that, as foreshadowed by the attack which the Ark Royal's Swordfish made on the Strasbourg on 3rd July, 1940, torpedoes dropped from the air could cripple capital ships at sea, even when protected by a screen of destroyers.

That opportunity came on 28th March, 1941, when an R.A.F. reconnaissance reported a force of Italian warships 100 miles east of Cape Passero in Sicily, steering to the eastward, with the probable object of attacking the British convoys that were on their way to Greece. The Mediterranean Fleet had left Alexandria to meet this threat, and at six o'clock next morning the aircraft-carrier Formidable (Captain, now Rear-Admiral, A. W. La Touche Bisset), which had recently joined the Fleet, flew off a reconnaissance of four Albacores and one Swordfish to search the area between Crete and Cyrenaica. The Formidable was wearing the flag of Rear-Admiral D. W. Boyd, who had relieved Rear-Admiral Lyster in command of Mediterranean Aircraft-carriers.

At 7.20 a.m. the most northerly aircraft of the search made an alarm report of cruisers and destroyers, amplified later to four cruisers and seven destroyers, to the south-west of Crete. The search was hampered by poor visibility and the presence of enemy aircraft.

The Italian cruisers were steering to the

south-east towards the Fleet. Vice-Admiral H. D. Pridham-Wippell, K.C.B., C.V.O., in command of Light Forces, with his flag in H.M.S. Orion, immediately advanced to meet them. At nine o'clock they were observed to turn to the westward, in an attempt (as became clear later) to lead the Vice-Admiral Light Forces towards the Italian flagship Vittorio Veneto. He sighted her two hours later, and was compelled to turn away to the southward to avoid being overwhelmed.

The Formidable had available ten Albacores, four Swordfish and thirteen Fulmars. At 10 a.m. she flew off a striking force of six Albacores, led by Lieutenant-Commander W. H. G. Saunt, D.S.C., R.N., and two Fulmars as escort, with orders to attack the enemy cruisers. An hour later, when 100 miles from the carrier, the striking force sighted a single capital ship steaming southeastward at high speed with a screen of four destroyers. At first they thought her to be a detached British battleship, but returned to her when they saw her engaging Admiral Pridham-Wippell's force. She was in fact the Vittorio Veneto. The destroyers were dispersed on her disengaged port side.

Lieutenant-Commander Saunt led his force on to her starboard bow and went in to the attack at 11.27 in two sub-flights. As the Albacores were peeling off to dive they were attacked by two Ju.88s. The Fulmar escort shot one down into the sea. The other made off. Seeing the direction of the attack, the destroyers moved over to the starboard side and the Vittorio Veneto made a wide turn to starboard. During the attack all the ships put up intense antiaircraft fire, and a splash barrage from the battleship's 15-inch shells was designed to swamp the aircraft while they were close to the water. As the Albacores broke away they dodged these splashes and there were no casualties. One certain hit was observed on the port quarter of the Vittorio Veneto. She began to lose speed and her steering gear appeared to be out of action. She

turned away to the westward, thus breaking off the engagement with the British cruisers but preventing Admiral Cunningham, in H.M.S. Warspite, from engaging her.

Meanwhile three Swordfish based at Maleme airfield in Crete had flown off to attack the Italian cruisers and sighted them at noon, steaming in line ahead with the screening destroyers. They attacked the rear cruiser out of the sun, but could observe no hits.

As soon as the Formidable's search aircraft returned to the ship they were refuelled and armed with torpedoes, and by noon a second striking force of three Albacores, two Swordfish, with two Fulmars as escort, was ranged. By that time the first striking force was ready to land on. The carrier hauled out of the line, escorted by two destroyers, flew off the second striking force and landed on the first, then turned to rejoin the Battle Squadron, which was by that time twelve miles ahead. While doing so she was attacked by two Italian S.M.79s, which made a low approach but dropped their torpedoes at a range of over 2,000 yards, so that the carrier had no difficulty in combing the tracks. Both torpedoes exploded harmlessly astern.

Admiral Cunningham retained the second striking force over the fleet for an hour, since he was hoping to engage the Vittorio Veneto. She had, however, still too great a lead, and at 1.50 the leader of the striking force, Lieutenant-Commander J. Dalyell Stead, R.N., was given her estimated position and sent off to the attack. At 3.25, to the south of Cape Matapan, he sighted her ahead, now screened by two destroyers on either bow. He worked up into the sun and brought the squadron down to 5,000 feet before being observed. The leading destroyer then opened fire, but the Fulmar escort compelled her to turn away.

The Vittorio Veneto took avoiding action by swinging 180 degrees to starboard. As she turned, the three Albacores of the first

MOMENT OF ATTACK AT MATAPAN. During the daylight of 28th March, 1941, torpedo-bombers of the Fleet Air Arm kept up a running fight with the enemy force, making five attacks in all. In the remarkable picture above, the leading Swordfish of a striking force based on Crete has been photographed from the second aircraft a few seconds after dropping its torpedo. The splash can be seen below the Swordfish. By an accident of photography the biplane looks like a monoplane. *Below*, Italian Bolzano class cruisers change course to evade another attack.

sub-flight attacked. The observers saw splashes on the port bow and amidships. By the time the two Swordfish reached the water the Vittorio Veneto had completed her turn and, dropping from perfect positions on her exposed starboard side, the crews observed two large splashes. As before, all the aircraft were imperilled by the splashes from the heavy guns, but all save the leader returned safely. There is no evidence to show how he was lost.

As a result of this attack the Vittorio Veneto's speed was further reduced to 13 knots. She continued to steer to the westward, but owing to the shortage of shadowing aircraft touch was lost for a while, although the pursuing Battle Squadron picked up her oil track for 15 miles. Then one of the three Albacores which had been flown off after returning from the first attack sighted her at 3 p.m. This aircraft continued to report her movements for over four hours until relieved by a night shadower. The Commander-in-Chief also sent out the flagship's special " action observation " Swordfish floatplane, which sighted the Vittorio Veneto at 6.20, and a separate group of enemy cruisers and destroyers a few minutes later. As the light began to fail both the Swordfish and the Albacore closed in to a mile astern. When the relief night shadower appeared, the Swordfish made for Suda Bay in Crete, having kept touch until well after sunset.

At dusk the Vittorio Veneto, although within sight of the cruisers, was still 40 miles ahead of the Battle Squadron, and it was decided to arm every available aircraft in the Formidable—six Albacores and two Swordfish—for a third attack, in the hope of catching her after sunset against the glow of the western horizon. While the striking force was being ranged, two Swordfish from Maleme sighted the Vittorio Veneto, which had been joined by other units of the Italian fleet. A further group of three cruisers, screened by four destroyers, was seen steering south to join them.

The Formidable's striking force made

TRYING TO TORPEDO THE FORMIDABLE. This Italian S.M. 79 has just dropped its torpedo at 2,000 yards range at the British aircraft-carrier. No harm was done.

contact with the Swordfish from Maleme and, directed by the shadowing aircraft, sighted the enemy five minutes before sunset. Lieutenant-Commander Saunt went into the attack at 7.25, by which time the cruisers from the northward had joined the Vittorio Veneto. The fleet was steaming in five columns, the damaged battleship in the centre, nursed by three cruisers on either side, and encircled by destroyers.

The striking force was received by a tremendous barrage over a wide arc astern of the fleet. The Commanding Officer of the Orion, watching from the bridge in the distance, said that he had never seen such a pyrotechnic display. The intensity of the fire forced the striking force to turn off to starboard. The formation broke up and each aircraft attacked independently between 7.30 and 7.45 from widely different angles. In addition to the danger from the barrage there were a number of narrow escapes from collision. A false cloud horizon in the west added to the difficulties of the attack. The majority of the pilots believed that they had dropped at the battleship, but the barrage, the smoke, and the searchlights which were flashing in all directions, made it extremely difficult to determine results.

To avoid confusing the attack the Swordfish from Maleme decided to follow in rear of the main striking force. Owing to the intensity of the barrage on the starboard side one pilot went in slowly on the port side to the edge of the smoke screen and dropped his torpedo at 1,000 yards. As he turned away, a large ship, accompanied by a destroyer, came out of the smoke in line with the torpedo, but it was impossible to observe whether he had scored a hit. The second Swordfish attacked towards the rear of the starboard column. He, too, was unable to observe results, and as he turned away the tail of his aircraft was hit.

One of the Formidable's pilots did not attack until 7.45, and it seems probable that either he or the second pilot from Maleme hit the cruiser Pola : it was subsequently confirmed that she was struck at 7.46. The damage she received stopped her engines and caused all her electric power to fail, rendering her a drifting hulk. This had important consequences, for the 10,000-ton cruisers Zara and Fiume were detached to help her, and both they and the Pola were sunk by the gunfire and torpedoes of the Battle Squadron during the night action which followed.

The captain of the Pola told an officer in the destroyer which rescued him later that night that he had never seen such courage as that displayed by the crew of the aircraft which attacked him, for they had approached only a few feet above the water to a very close range in the face of a withering fire. " I can only call it an act of God," he said.

All the aircraft in the dusk attack returned safely to Maleme with the exception of one which, owing to petrol shortage, landed in the Kithera Channel near H.M.S. Juno, which rescued the crew. The night-shadowing aircraft crashed in Suda Bay while trying to land, but the crew were picked up unhurt. Next morning two searches were sent out to locate the damaged Vittorio Veneto, but all they sighted were boats and rafts with survivors from the ships which had been destroyed. The aircraft led the Fleet to the nearest of them, but the destroyers' work of rescue was interrupted by the attacks of the German bombers.

The Battle of Matapan had results that were even more important than the damage to the Vittorio Veneto and the sinking of the three Italian cruisers and two destroyers, for it enabled Admiral Cunningham to transport the expeditionary force to Greece, and later to evacuate it, without interference from the Italian fleet. The result would not have been achieved without the work of the naval aircraft engaged, but the Formidable had not enough aircraft to maintain continuous touch with the separate Italian forces and at the same time build up the striking force necessary to sink or stop a modern capital ship. That triumph was to be reserved for the aircraft of the Victorious and the Ark Royal.

On 22nd May, 1941, Vice-Admiral Sir John Tovey, K.C.B., D.S.O., acting on the report of the Maryland which had made the reconnaissance to Bergen, made dispositions to prevent the Bismarck and the Prinz Eugen from breaking out into the Atlantic, and put to sea with the Home Fleet, flying his flag in H.M.S. King George V. With him he had H.M.S. Victorious (Captain H. C. Bovell, R.N.), a new carrier, which had only recently been commissioned and had been about to sail from Scapa with a large consignment of dismantled Hurricanes for Gibraltar, where they were to be assembled and flown to the R.A.F. at Malta. She also had on board nine Swordfish and six Fulmars. She had had only a week to work up their crews, who were still unused to flying as a squadron.

On the evening of 23rd May the cruisers Suffolk and Norfolk sighted the enemy ships steering to the south-west in the Denmark Strait, between Greenland and Iceland, and shadowed them throughout the night. Shortly after daylight on the 24th the Hood and the Prince of Wales brought the Bismarck to action. The Hood was sunk and the Prince of Wales slightly damaged. The chase continued.

The Commander-in-Chief was steaming at 27 knots to intercept the Bismarck, but it was essential to reduce her speed if she were to be brought to action, and during the afternoon of the 24th he detached the Victorious from his main force, with an escort of four cruisers, to reach a position within aircraft striking distance of the enemy. This force was commanded by Rear-Admiral A. T. B. Curteis, with his flag in H.M.S. Galatea.

In the high latitude south of the Denmark Strait sunset was not until an hour after midnight, so that it was still light when the striking force, the whole squadron of nine Swordfish, led by Lieutenant-Commander (A) E. Esmonde, R.N., flew off at 10.10 p.m. to avenge the Hood. It was followed at

THE HUNTERS. The Bismarck is being chased. It is 24th May, 1941. The Victorious is racing to get within striking distance. Ranged aft on the wet flight-deck. the Swordfish wait for the order to take off.

11 p.m. by three Fulmars, and by two more at 1 a.m. as reliefs. Their duty was to maintain touch with the Bismarck so that a second attack might be launched at dawn.

The weather was showery, with squalls, and a fresh north-westerly wind. Visibility was good, except during the showers. By expert navigation the striking force sighted the Bismarck at 11.30 p.m., 120 miles from the carrier. Lieutenant-Commander Esmonde altered course with the intention of making his attack from ahead. The cloud was increasing and he lost touch, but after circling round he made visual contact with the Norfolk, which informed him that the enemy was to his north-west. A few minutes later he broke cloud cover to attack, only to find himself over a United States coastguard cutter. The Bismarck, then no more than six miles away, sighted the aircraft as they came out of the cloud and opened with a barrage of anti-aircraft fire, which remained intense throughout the attack, the short-range armament coming into action as the aircraft closed. So accurate was it that Lieutenant-Commander Esmonde's Swordfish was hit at a range of four miles.

Nevertheless, soon after midnight he led the first sub-flight straight through that barrier of fire. His starboard lower aileron was hit, and he abandoned his original intention of attacking the Bismarck on the starboard side, deciding to drop while he was in a good position on the port bow. Lieutenant P. D. Gick, R.N., who was leading the second sub-flight, was not satisfied with his first approach: he took the sub-flight away from the heaviest part of the barrage, and by keeping low over the water worked his way to a better position. Lieutenant (A) H. C. M. Pollard, R.N., led the third sub-flight round the ship and pressed home the attack, where the fire was less intense. One aircraft of this sub-flight became detached in cloud and failed to find the target. As the Swordfish turned away the air-gunners sprayed the Bismarck's superstructure and gun positions with machine-gun fire at almost point-blank range.

The striking force was able to claim one definite hit on the Bismarck. Several witnesses had seen a column of water rise

THE HUNTED SHIP. It is just after the Northern midnight. From a Swordfish about to drop to the attack the Bismarck is seen in the twilight through the rain clouds driving low over a sea whipped by a squally north-west wind. She was struck by a torpedo amidships.

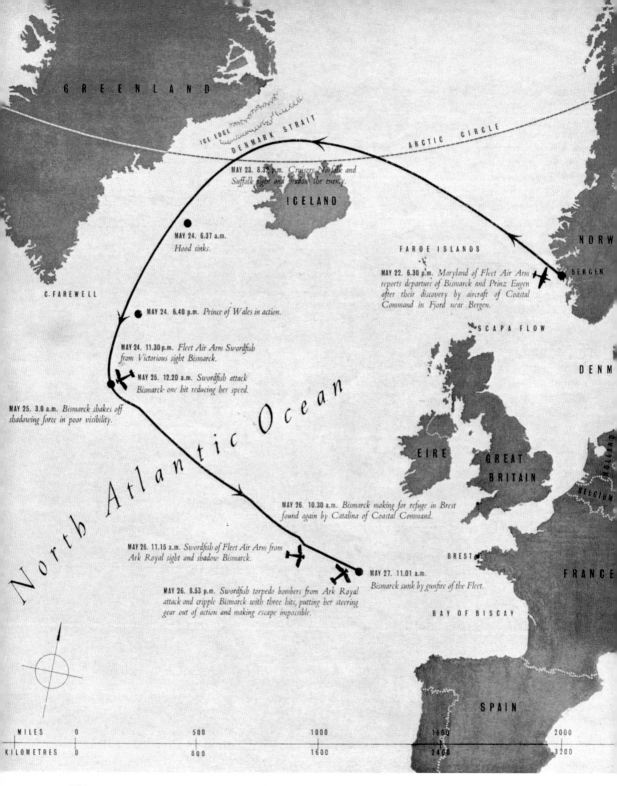

GREENLAND

DENMARK STRAIT

ICE EDGE

ARCTIC CIRCLE

ICELAND

MAY 23. 8.32 p.m. *Cruisers Norfolk and Suffolk sight and shadow the enemy.*

FAROE ISLANDS

NORW

BERGEN

MAY 24. 6.37 a.m. *Hood sinks.*

MAY 22. 6.30 p.m. *Maryland of Fleet Air Arm reports departure of Bismarck and Prinz Eugen after their discovery by aircraft of Coastal Command in Fjord near Bergen.*

C. FAREWELL

SCAPA FLOW

MAY 24. 6.40 p.m. *Prince of Wales in action.*

DENM

MAY 24. 11.30 p.m. *Fleet Air Arm Swordfish from Victorious sight Bismarck.*

MAY 25. 12.20 a.m. *Swordfish attack Bismarck- one hit reducing her speed.*

MAY 25. 3.0 a.m. *Bismarck shakes off shadowing force in poor visibility.*

EIRE

GREAT
BRITAIN

HOLLAND

North Atlantic Ocean

BELGIUM

MAY 26. 10.30 a.m. *Bismarck making for refuge in Brest found again by Catalina of Coastal Command.*

MAY 26. 11.15 a.m. *Swordfish of Fleet Air Arm from Ark Royal sight and shadow Bismarck.*

BREST

FRANCE

MAY 27. 11.01 a.m. *Bismarck sunk by gunfire of the Fleet.*

MAY 26. 8.53 p.m. *Swordfish torpedo bombers from Ark Royal attack and cripple Bismarck with three hits, putting her steering gear out of action and making escape impossible.*

BAY OF BISCAY

SPAIN

MILES	0		500		1000		1500		2000
KILOMETRES	0		800		1600		2400		3200

THE CHASE AND DESTRUCTION OF THE BISMARCK.

into the air amidships, followed by heavy black and white smoke ; the observers estimated that her speed had been effectively reduced. Lieutenant-Commander Esmonde signalled to the Victorious : " Have attacked with torpedoes. Only one observed."

By that time the weather had become worse, and the clouds were hanging low over the sea. Rear-Admiral Curteis had been steaming to the westward to shorten the return journey of the striking force. Even so, it was a wonder to all on board that any of the aircraft returned to the carrier. As they were coming in, a violent rain squall struck the ship, so that they missed her in the darkness. It was with relief that the Air Staff Officer heard the first plaintive call of a Swordfish asking for bearings. They were homed back by searchlights, and by 2.30 a.m. all had landed on, many uncomfortably close to the limit of their endurance. Three of the pilots made their first night deck-landing with complete success.

The Fulmars were less fortunate. Night shadowing is a task which tries the most experienced of crews, and it was through no lack of gallantry that they failed to hold the Bismarck long on so rough a night. Two of the Fulmars were lost, but the crew of one, after many hours in their dinghy, were rescued by a merchant ship, S.S. Ravenhill.

Lieutenant-Commander Esmonde and his companions had cause for jubilation in the great ante-room of the Victorious on their return. They had not sunk the Bismarck, it was true, but they had hit her. The extent of the damage they could not tell, but they believed (rightly) that they had reduced her speed, and they were eagerly looking forward to the chance of finishing her off when daylight came.

" This attack, by a squadron so lately embarked in a new carrier," wrote the Commander-in-Chief in his despatch, " in unfavourable weather conditions, was magnificently carried out and reflects the greatest credit on all concerned. There can be little doubt that the hit was largely responsible

BEARING GREAT NEWS. Swordfish from the Ark Royal are seen from the Sheffield as they return to their carrier on 26th May. The Bismarck is doomed. She has been crippled by three more torpedo hits.

for the Bismarck being finally brought to action and sunk."

Nevertheless the Bismarck was not finished yet, and she succeeded in eluding her pursuers for a time. At 3 a.m. on the morning of 25th May—three hours after the attack—the cruisers which had been tracking her for over 1,000 miles lost touch in the darkness. It was, therefore, impossible for Captain Bovell to fly off the dawn striking force as he had planned. Instead, the Swordfish were sent out to search the sea, but they too failed to find her. Two of them did not return to the ship. One crew remained at sea in their dinghy until 3rd June, when they were picked up by a trawler 50 miles east of Cape Farewell and were landed in Iceland. The other crew, having flown for five hours and ten minutes until their fuel gave out, landed on the sea near an abandoned lifeboat from a Norwegian steamer. They found it well stocked with provisions and water, and after spending seven days aboard were picked up off the coast of Greenland by a steamer bound from the United States to Iceland.

The search for the Bismarck lasted until 10.30 on the morning of 26th May, when a Catalina of Coastal Command sighted her steaming in the direction of Brest. She drove the Catalina off by anti-aircraft fire, but a few minutes later a Swordfish from H.M.S. Ark Royal, which had been steaming at high speed from Gibraltar with Force H, sighted her and shadowed her with its fellows until another striking force could be despatched.

The story of how the Ark Royal completed the work which the Victorious had begun has already been related in " Ark Royal "

(*H.M.S.O.*). It is enough to say that a striking force of 15 Swordfish, led by Lieutenant-Commander T. P. Coode, R.N., flying in even worse weather, attacked the Bismarck at 8.53 p.m. on the 26th and obtained three hits, damaging her steering gear and further reducing her speed, thus enabling the Commander-in-Chief to bring her to action and destroy her next morning.

10. THE GALLANT SORTIE

SHORTLY after the destruction of the Bismarck, Lieutenant-Commander Esmonde's squadron was transferred to the Ark Royal, and was with her when she was sunk by a torpedo from a German submarine in the Mediterranean on 13th November, 1941. Lieutenant-Commander Esmonde left the sinking ship with Captain Maund, and later reformed the squadron at Lee-on-Solent, with seven of the officers who had been in the Ark. The squadron was reduced from nine Swordfish to six, and had seven pilots, six observers and six telegraphist-air-gunners. Two of the pilots had but recently finished their training. Only two of the observers had had operational experience. All the air-gunners came from the Victorious, and one, Leading Airman A. L. Johnson, had been awarded the D.S.M. after the Bismarck attack.

What the squadron officers lacked in experience they made up for in enthusiasm, and they had a squadron commander of. proved ability who had that rare quality of inspiring in others a devotion to duty equal to his own.

The squadron was to be sent to one of the new escort carriers which were then expected from the United States, and at the beginning of February, 1942, it was preparing to move to H.M.S. Landrail for working up. Two

of the squadron officers had gone on ahead, but were suddenly recalled.

The Admiralty appreciated that the Scharnhorst, Gneisenau and Prinz Eugen might break out from Brest and attempt to force a passage through the Channel to their home ports. The Fleet Air Arm had a long account to settle with the Scharnhorst and Gneisenau. Eight of the Ark Royal's Skua crews had perished in the attack on the Scharnhorst at Trondheim and two Swordfish in the attack off the Norwegian coast ; and although naval aircraft had sighted the two ships more than once in the Atlantic, no striking force had ever caught them. Here was the chance, and it was characteristic of Esmonde that he asked to be allowed to lead his squadron against them, should the need for a striking force arise. That request was granted, and he was told that if he went he would be given every possible support.

One evening some of the squadron officers returned from a visit to the pictures at Lee to be called to Esmonde's cabin. He told them to be in readiness for a strike at any moment. The aircraft were prepared and armed with torpedoes. There was a " flap " at 3 a.m. next morning and the officers were briefed, but it was a false alarm—a few enemy trawlers sighted in the Channel.

Next morning the squadron flew to an R.A.F. station in Kent, where it arrived in a blizzard. The maintenance ratings followed by lorry. The squadron was then at five minutes' readiness. It is necessary to emphasise the fact that Esmonde was expecting to make a night attack, and arrangements had been made for R.A.F. fighters to accompany the Swordfish as flare-droppers. The officers had been told the objective under the seal of secrecy ; Esmonde had written it on a piece of paper, which he burnt after they had read it. As there were seven pilots and only six Swordfish, the two juniors tossed to decide who should go.

The maintenance ratings behaved magnificently. They had to dig the dispersed aircraft out of the snow in the morning and run the engines up three times during the day to keep them warm. The gunner (T.), who had come with the squadron from Lee, although a sick man, serviced the torpedoes night and day until he collapsed.

On 11th February Esmonde went to Buckingham Palace to attend the investiture and to receive the D.S.O. he had been awarded for the Bismarck action. Next morning, Thursday, 12th February, Sub-Lieutenant (A) B. W. Rose, R.N.V.R., was returning to the mess with his observer after a practice flight, when a lorry with some of the squadron officers came tearing past. One of them shouted, " The balloon's gone up ! " It was then a few minutes after noon.

Rose and his observer ran back to the crew room and put on their flying kit again. Just as they were ready, Esmonde came rushing in.

" The Scharnhorst, Gneisenau and Prinz Eugen have had the cheek to put their noses out into the Channel, and we're going out to deal with them," he said. " Fly at 50 feet, close line astern, individual attacks, and find your own way home. We shall have fighter protection."

The crews got into their aircraft, taxied out, took off at 12.30, formed up in Vic., and circled over the airfield for three minutes. Then a squadron of ten Spitfires came out. As soon as Esmonde saw them he led the first sub-flight off to the attack in line astern, followed by the second, led by Lieutenant Thomson, in V formation.

By that time the German warships had passed through the Straits of Dover and were about ten miles north of Calais. According to the German account, they had left Brest immediately after an R.A.F. raid at 8.30 on the previous night, with an escort of destroyers. At dawn a large number of E-boats and minesweepers had joined the squadron, which had proceeded up Channel hugging the French coast, covered by an umbrella of shore-based fighters which could be relieved and reinforced from the coastal airfields at short notice : the biggest fighter screen ever seen over a naval force. As the squadron passed through the Straits the long-range batteries on the Kentish coast opened fire, but the ships were able to take evasive action, and were also able to avoid the torpedoes fired by the British motor boats and destroyers which tried to intercept them.

When the striking force sighted the enemy after 20 minutes' flying, the ships were a mile and a half away, steaming in line ahead, the Prinz Eugen leading, followed by the Scharnhorst and the Gneisenau. They were almost through the Straits and the crews of the Swordfish could see the splashes of the shells from the shore batteries. Visibility had been patchy during the passage of the striking force, sometimes right down, at other times two miles. The Spitfire escort had to weave widely to avoid losing touch with the slow Swordfish.

The striking force went in to the attack over the destroyer screen. As they closed in towards the capital ships they were met with intense anti-aircraft fire. While Esmonde was still flying at 50 feet a shell ricochetted off the water and hit his aircraft, causing him to steer an erratic course.

Johnson, the air-gunner of Rose's Swordfish, next astern, was hit.

Then the ships' guns calmed down and the fighter attacks began. About 15 Me. 109s and Focke-Wulf 190s dived out of the clouds on to the tails of the Swordfish. The Spitfire escort became involved in a general dog-fight. A Focke-Wulf 190 ripped off the top of the main plane of Esmonde's aircraft and he went straight down into the sea.

Rose was attacked both from ahead and astern, at a range of about 200 yards. He dodged as well as he could, his observer, Sub-Lieutenant (A) E. Lee, R.N.V.R., standing up in the after cockpit and shouting " Port "—" Starboard " as the attacks came in. They could see the tracer bullets streaming past, and the Swordfish was being hit continually. The constant evasive action slowed the advance of the Swordfish, and to make matters worse there was no one to work the rear gun, for Johnson had either been knocked unconscious or killed instantaneously, and Lee could not move his body.

In spite of Lee's watchfulness, Rose was hit at length by splinters from a cannon shell which struck the bulkhead behind his seat. He was now leading, and decided he must attack without delay, since his engine was faltering. He selected the leading ship and, getting as good a position as he could, he dropped his torpedo at a range of about 1,200 yards and saw it running well. It was difficult to observe results, but directly he had made his attack the fighters ceased to pay any further attention to him and concentrated on the others. One Swordfish had two Focke-Wulfs on its tail, their flaps and undercarriages down to retard their speed, attacking whichever way the pilot turned.

The third aircraft of the sub-flight, piloted by Sub-Lieutenant (A) C. M. Kingsmill, R.N.V.R., had the two top cylinders of its engine shot away ; the engine and the upper port wing caught fire. The air-gunner, Leading Airman D. A. Bunce, continued to engage the enemy fighters and saw one crash into the sea. Although all the crew were wounded Kingsmill kept control of his aircraft long enough to aim his torpedo in the direction of the second enemy ship, then turned with difficulty and tried to land near some vessels which turned out to be E-boats. They opened fire on him, but he kept flying until his engine finally cut. The Swordfish crashed on the water a few hundred yards from some British motor torpedo-boats, which rescued the crew, who had taken to the water, their dinghy having been destroyed by fire.

The three Swordfish in the second subflight, piloted by Lieutenant (A) J. C. Thompson, R.N., Sub-Lieutenant (A) C. R. Wood, R.N., and Sub-Lieutenant (A) P. Bligh, R.N.V.R., were last seen crossing the destroyer screen to attack. They were taking violent evasive action, but were proceeding steadily towards the capital ships. Nothing further is known of them.

As soon as Rose had dropped his torpedo he tried to make as much height as possible and went out on the port wing of the destroyer screen. He had got up to 1,200 feet when Lee told him that petrol was pouring out of the starboard side. It was obvious that he could not reach the English coast and he decided to make for some motor torpedo-boats. When he was within four miles of them his engine cut. He glided down towards the sea, pulled his stick well back and pancaked. As he said later, " The Swordfish sat down very nicely."

He climbed out of his cockpit into the sea. Lee tried to remove Johnson, the air-gunner, from the after cockpit, but found it impossible. Rose could not help him because his left arm was useless. The dinghy (kept in the top of the main plane and automatically blown up) was washed into the sea. Rose recovered it and got it upright. Lee held it while Rose climbed into it, then went back to the aircraft to make another attempt to remove Johnson. He could not do so, and had to leave him. There was no doubt that he was dead.

Lee then joined Rose in the dinghy. The sea was choppy and the dinghy was soon full of water. They used their flying helmets for baling, but without much success. Then they hauled in the waterproof bag with the emergency gear which was attached to the dinghy and took out the marine distress signals and the aluminium dust-markers— the dust forms a silver pool round the dinghy which can be seen at a distance. But they flung the dust to windward and it blew back on them, so that they looked like a couple of shining tin soldiers.

They used the empty tins for baling out the dinghy and when they had got it dry they fired the distress signals. Two motor torpedo-boats closed in on the dinghy, which by that time had been an hour and a half in the water.

At first Rose and Lee feared that the M.T.Bs. might be E-boats, and were relieved to hear an English voice hailing them. One of the boats came alongside and Lee got on board. A rating jumped in and helped Rose out : he was suffering severely from his wounds, which it had been impossible to dress in the dinghy, and both he and Lee were numb with cold.

There were only five survivors from the striking force. Lee was the only one un-wounded. Having made his report to the naval authorities, he apologised for having to hurry away, but he was, he explained, now Acting Senior Officer of the little squadron.

The four surviving officers were awarded the D.S.O., the air-gunner, Leading Airman Bunce, the C.G.M. The crews who lost their lives received mentions in despatches, the only posthumous honour possible save the Victoria Cross, which was bestowed upon Lieutenant-Commander Esmonde, the first member of the Fleet Air Arm to receive it.

" In my opinion," wrote Vice-Admiral B. H. Ramsay, the Flag Officer Commanding Dover, " the gallant sortie of these six Sword-fish constitutes one of the finest exhibitions of self-sacrifice and devotion to duty that the war has yet witnessed."

At the time of the action much was said, and written, on the folly of sending out-of-date Swordfish aircraft on so hazardous a task. This is not the place to discuss what should not have been done, or what was left undone, and the engagement has been the subject of an enquiry, the findings of which, as the Prime Minister has stated, are unlikely to be disclosed until after the war.

But this at least may be said : Eugene Esmonde was a brave man and an inspiring leader ; he was also a pilot of exceptional experience. He was too wise a captain, and he had too much integrity, to waste either his crews' lives or his own in an attack which held no hope of success. He was free to act as he thought best, and believed that he might succeed. That he was taking tremendous risks he knew, but he was pre-pared to face them, as he had faced other risks many times before.

The break-out of the German warships was astutely planned and boldly executed. It is true that those six Davids of the Fleet Air Arm proved no match for the three German Goliaths with their helmets of fighter air-craft, but it would be less than just to say that their mission failed. Failure, even though it may be not without honour, is a melancholy word, but success is not always the full measure of glory. There are so-called failures which will live in history when victories are forgotten. The charge of the Light Brigade at Balaclava was one of them. The sortie of Esmonde's Swordfish beyond the Straits of Dover was another.

The heights to which the human spirit may rise are unpredictable, and the effort of the will, which is the weapon of the spirit, transcends failure or success. That morning Esmonde and his companions created an imperishable example which will live in the traditions of the Royal Navy and will remain for future generations a fine and stirring memory. Thirteen of the squadron gave their lives. In the hearts of those who returned there is no bitterness.

" I know that if Winkle Esmonde were alive and the same call came again, he would not hesitate to form another striking force," said one of them. " And we would follow him."

ESCORT I

THE SKY: THE FIGHTERS

11. "WE WILL GO UP AND FIGHT."

" WE will go up and fight " : to-day, the old battle-cry from the Book of Deuteronomy is echoed by the naval pilots who fly the Fulmars, Martlets, Sea-Hurricanes and Sea-fires which operate with the Fleet.

The functions of the carrier-borne fighters are primarily to protect, as when they form a defensive umbrella over a naval force or a convoy of merchant ships, or escort a striking force of torpedo-aircraft. They were, however, used offensively during the Norwegian campaign and in other combined operations.

The first naval fighters to fulfil their protective duties were three of the now obsolete Skuas from the Ark Royal. On 26th September, 1939, while the Fleet was escorting a damaged submarine across the North Sea, Lieutenant B. S. McEwen, R.N., and his air-gunner, Petty Officer Airman B. M. Seymour, shot down a Dornier 18 flying-boat shadower. This was the first enemy aircraft to be destroyed in the war.

Between October, 1939, and March, 1940, shore-based Skuas, Rocs and Gladiators defended the Fleet Base at Scapa. They had a number of combats with German bombers, shooting down two, and four probables, without loss, and on Christmas Day, 1940, the first combat of the American Grumman Martlets resulted in two of them, piloted by Lieutenant L. V. Carver, R.N., and Sub-Lieutenant (A) Parke, R.N.V.R., forcing down a Ju. 88 which was coming in to attack the Fleet. The crew of four were captured.

The work of the shore-based fighters in Crete and the Western Desert will be described in a later chapter, but others fought side by side with the R.A.F. squadrons in the Battle of Britain.

After the evacuation of Dunkirk, when the Luftwaffe's attack on Great Britain was imminent, the Admiralty offered the Air Ministry the loan of any naval pilots under training (with the exception of executive officers) who would volunteer. There were then two courses—about 40 pilots—at the Fighter School in H.M.S. Raven. All the officers under instruction volunteered for temporary service with the R.A.F. and were sent to operational training units for a course in flying Hurricanes and Spitfires. There they were taught by experienced fighter pilots just back from France, who were able to pass on their hardly-won knowledge of German tactics in air combat. In July, 1940, having completed the course, the naval pilots were posted to R.A.F. fighter squadrons. They retained their naval uniforms and were paid by the Admiralty, but for discipline and operational purposes they were under the squadrons to which they were attached, and, as casualties occurred, many of them became section-leaders and led R.A.F. officers.

Three of these pilots joined the front-line Hurricane squadron which had recently returned from France and had been re-formed at an East Anglian station by Squadron Leader Douglas Bader. This indomitable fighter, whose prowess became legendary before he was made a prisoner of war, created a magnificent spirit in the squadron, which began operations with convoy patrols off the East Coast. The first victim fell to one of the naval pilots, Sub-Lieutenant (A) R. E. Gardner, R.N., who shot down a Ju. 88 in mid-July, having chased it 50 miles out to sea. Midshipman Patterson was killed early in the operations, but Sub-Lieutenant (A) R. J. Cork, R.N., the third of the trio, brought down his first German on the afternoon of 30th August, when between 75 and 100 Heinkels and Messerschmitts came over. That was the squadron's first big day : it accounted for twelve German aircraft.

On 7th September, while the squadron

was climbing up over the North Weald, Cork, flying in company with Bader, suddenly saw about 100 Do. 17s and Me. 110s far above them. Bader opened to full throttle and climbed to get underneath them. He, Cork, and one other pilot flew far ahead of the squadron. They encountered cross-fire from the enemy bombers, which kept in perfect formation, and at the same time the Messerschmitts, which had the advantage of 4,000 feet in height, attacked from astern, out of the sun. Tracers were coming down like streams of milk. The third pilot was shot down, but Bader and Cork, although their aircraft were badly hit, continued to climb steeply until each was able to get in one long burst. Cork fired at a Dornier on the tail end of the formation. Its port engine burst into flames. Then he was attacked from astern by an enemy fighter, who hit his starboard main plane. He broke away downwards and nearly collided head-on with another Me. 110. Before pulling away he gave it a short burst and saw the front of the cabin break up. It went into a vertical dive. Both the crew baled out. Cork was following the Messerschmitt, which was stalling, when he was attacked astern by another. A cannon shell went through the side of his hood, hit the bottom of the reflector sight, then the bullet-proof windscreen.

" I received a certain number of glass splinters in my eyes from the windscreen," he wrote in his report, " and as I could not see very well, broke away downwards with a half roll, and lost enemy machine."

That day the squadron accounted for ten German aircraft, but eight days later, on 15th September, the peak day of the Battle of Britain, when the R.A.F. destroyed 185, the squadron's share of the bag was 25. In the first foray, about noon, Cork brought down another Do. 17 in what Bader described as " the finest shambles I have been in." In the afternoon, over the Thames Estuary, the squadron engaged another formation of Dorniers and Messer-

schmitts. This is an extract from Sub-Lieutenant Cork's combat report :

" Whilst flying as Red 2 in the leading section of the squadron we sighted the enemy to the south and well above us. We climbed as fast as possible to the attack, but on the way were attacked from above and behind by a number of Me. 109s. The order was given on R/T to break formation, so I broke sharply away with a Me. on my tail. I was now in a dive and suddenly flew through the second squadron in the Wing formation and lost the enemy machine ; at the same time I saw a Do. 17 on my starboard, flying N.W. I dived 6,000 feet to attack and fired a long burst at the port engine, which started to smoke. I attacked again on the beam— large pieces of enemy machine flew off and his starboard wing burst into flames near the wing tip. He dived straight into the cloud, heading towards a clear patch, so I waited till he came into the open and fired another burst in a head-on attack and the machine dived into the ground.

" I climbed up 1,000 feet and was attacked by two yellow-nosed Me. 109s from above, so I did a steep turn to left and managed to get on the tail of one, fired a very short burst, and then ran out of ammunition. No damage was seen on enemy machine, but as I was being attacked from behind by a second fighter I went into a vertical dive down to 2,000 feet and returned to base. No damage to my own machine."

Meanwhile the other naval pilots were achieving success in the squadrons to which they were attached. Sub-Lieutenant (A) F. Dawson Paul, R.N.V.R., brought down five Germans during July alone. All expressed the greatest admiration for the men with whom they flew. " They were the grandest crowd of chaps I have ever known, with a wizard C.O.," wrote one who had joined Squadron Leader Joslin's squadron, near Dover.

The following is this officer's account of his first combat :—

" For the first time the Hun appeared in

large numbers and in broad daylight. We (three of us) were directed over the Channel to meet a reported 50 plus of aircraft. We climbed rapidly to 20,000 feet, and then I saw them in the bright blue of the sky— three solitary white trails coming out of a high layer of cloud, and growing steadily longer. They were some 4,000 feet above us. We gave our Hurricanes everything they had and climbed up towards them. Instead of attacking us they climbed rapidly and went into a defensive circle, making no attempt to attack. We reached them at last at 32,000 feet, our Hurricanes on the point of stall and with no manœuvrability at all. Still they did not attempt to attack us, although they had manœuvrability and about twelve times our number. We separated and I flew inside their circle, in the opposite direction to them, and waited until one flew into my sights. I fired and the recoil immediately stalled me and I started to spin. I got out in about 2,000 feet, and looking about me found there wasn't an aircraft in the sky ; in 30 seconds some 40 aircraft had completely disappeared and I had the sky to myself.

" I think after the excitement and the exertion at that height I was a bit dazy, anyway I was rudely awakened by long flickering streams of tracer which seemed uncommonly near my head. Then he shot by in a steep dive, a lean black little blighter —my first 109. I dived as hard as I could make my Hurricane, at any moment expecting a wing to break off, and still the 109 drew away. Suddenly, near the French coast, he started to level off, and, quite satisfied apparently that he was safe, headed over the town of Calais. I got my sight on him, pressed, saw flickering tendrils reach out from my wings to his tail, saw a large piece come adrift and slip by me. Smoke started to trail, then crumpled, and I seemed to do a complete somersault. Flak had opened up at me, despite their own machine. I shot off home as fast as I could, having gained my first probable."

The naval pilots who survived the Battle of Britain left the R.A.F. squadrons in December, 1940 : they were but few. It is well to put on record their achievement, and the Fleet Air Arm's contribution to the saving of England. Small though the contribution may have been in numbers, it was great in spirit.

One of those survivors, Sub-Lieutenant M. A. Birrell, R.N., had the experience of being the first pilot to be shot from a catapult-armed merchantman in a Hurricane. The Admiralty introduced these vessels (which were known as C.A.M. ships) in the spring of 1941 for the protection of convoys against the menace of the long-range Focke-Wulf Kuriers which were co-operating with the U-boats in the Atlantic. The first few appointments were filled by volunteers from the Fleet Air Arm, and maintenance ratings were carried to service the aircraft. The Hurricane could be of use only while the convoy was within range of the Focke-Wulfs, a zone 600 miles off the Western Approaches. It was perilous work. After the presence of the enemy had been detected the Hurricane would be catapulted off, and when it had shot down the shadower, or driven it away, it had either to fly back to shore, or, if the distance were too great for its endurance, the pilot would either bale out or make a forced landing alongside the nearest ship and trust to being picked up.

The first of these ships, S.S. Michael E, sighted no hostile aircraft while passing through the danger zone on her passage in a convoy across the Atlantic, but on the fourth day she was torpedoed and sunk by a U-boat. The survivors were picked up after 20 hours in the boats, but the Hurricane was lost. Other C.A.M. ships followed, pilots being subsequently drawn from the R.A.F.

Concurrently with the C.A.M. ships the Admiralty fitted out, in the summer of 1941, a small fleet of naval catapult ships to escort convoys through the danger zone. For a time the aged Pegasus was thus employed. Some were requisitioned vessels of the Elders

GUARDIAN HURRICANE. From catapults such as this, fighter aircraft were launched from merchant ships to deal with bombing attacks on convoys. The Admiralty introduced them early in 1941. The first pilots were volunteers from the Fleet Air Arm.

and Fyffe's Line, which had carried bananas from the West Indies to Bristol before the war. They flew the White Ensign, but many of the ships' companies, often including the R.N.R. masters and chief engineers, were of the peace-time complement. They rendered gallant service at a time when the shortage of escort vessels was acute.

One was the Ariguani, long familiar to travellers in the Caribbean. On Sub-Lieutenant Birrell's return after being torpedoed he embarked in her with a Fulmar and sailed to escort another convoy across the Atlantic. While chasing a Focke-Wulf 400 miles off the Irish coast in August, 1941, he ran into foul weather and finally, his petrol exhausted, forced-landed on an airfield under construction in Londonderry. As he came down, the Northern Irish navvies, exasperated at his sudden advent into their midst, sent a shower of picks and shovels after the Fulmar, whose engine cut for good half-way along the unfinished runway. The last of his troubles was when an irate R.A.F. officer expostulated with him for landing on an unfinished airfield and told him to sheer off. As soon as the position was explained, however, he affably produced ham-and-eggs and beer, had the Fulmar refuelled, and Sub-Lieutenant Birrell and his observer returned to their base.

The first aircraft from one of these naval catapult ships to bring down a Focke-Wulf was an early-type Hurricane piloted by Lieutenant (A) R. W. H. Everett, R.N.V.R., from H.M.S. Maplin, on 3rd August, 1941. While the Maplin was on her way to pick up a convoy she sighted a Focke-Wulf low on the horizon ten miles astern, doubtless intent upon the same purpose. Six minutes later, as the convoy hove in view, Lieutenant Everett was catapulted off to engage the enemy.

" I got within one and a half miles of the Focke-Wulf before it seemed to notice my presence," he wrote in his combat report. " I intercepted it after nine minutes' flying and ranged up alongside at 600 yards and slightly above it. When my machine was slightly ahead of its starboard quarter the stern cannon opened fire. These rounds passed underneath or fell short of the Hurricane. It took quite an appreciable time to get abeam and the for'ard cannon was also firing—again the rounds passed underneath or short. The Focke-Wulf then turned sharply to port, but seemed to change its mind and turned back on its original course. By this time I had reached its starboard bow and three machine-guns opened up, as well as the for'ard cannon. I did a quick turn to port and opened fire just abaft the beam.

I fired five-second bursts all the way until I was 40 yards astern of the enemy. Another short burst at this range and my guns were empty. I noticed pieces flying off the starboard side of the Focke-Wulf and it appeared to be alight inside the fuselage. I broke away to port at 30 yards. My windshield and hood were covered with oil and I quickly jumped to the conclusion that my engine oil system was badly hit."

Although Lieutenant Everett did not realise it at the time, the oil came from the Focke-Wulf, which a few seconds later dived into the sea.

" My forward view was very obscured owing to oil," the report continues. " My one idea was to get down while I still had charge of the situation. I made two rather half-hearted attempts to bale out, but the machine nosed down and caught me when half out. I changed my mind and decided to land in the sea near H.M.S. Wanderer, and did so. The ship sent a boat and I was extremely well looked after."

One may imagine the scene as the destroyer's Ward Room toasted this very gallant pilot, who had, incidentally, won the Grand National on Gregalach in 1929. The Admiralty recognised his achievement by

AUXILIARY CARRIER. Converted in 1941 from a captured German vessel, H.M.S. Audacity was the first of a new type of small carrier. She had no hangar ; her six Martlet aircraft being parked aft.

the award of the D.S.O. He lost his life while ferrying an aircraft from Liverpool to Belfast in January, 1942.

An improvement on the naval catapult ships was the small carrier, H.M.S. Audacity, an ex-German steamer of 5,600 tons which the cruiser Dunedin had intercepted earlier in the war. There was a grim fitness in converting her for action against the U-boats' air-borne scouts.

When completed, the Audacity (Commander D. M. McKendrick, R.N., an old Swordfish pilot), had a flight-deck 420 feet in length and 60 feet in beam, but no hangar. The six Martlets which she carried were parked aft, so that the foremost aircraft had only 300 feet of runway. It says much for the skill of the first eight pilots who embarked in her that five had never previously landed on a carrier's deck.

The Audacity's first trip was in September, 1941, escorting an outward-bound Gibraltar convoy. The first excitement was on the 19th when the Martlets found a U-boat on the surface, and machine-gunned it until it submerged. On the following night U-boats sank several small vessels in the convoy. The survivors were taken aboard the rescue ship, Walmar Castle, which was bombed next morning by a Focke-Wulf and set on fire. Sub-Lieutenant (A) N. H. Patterson, R.N., and Sub-Lieutenant (A) G. R. P. Fletcher, R.N.V.R., attacked the Focke-Wulf and brought it down ; after they had given it 35 rounds from each gun the tail unit fell off and it dived into the sea. The only thing that came up was a pair of flying overalls.

One morning two Martlets were sent up to investigate an unidentified aircraft approaching the convoy at 8,000 feet, well out in the Atlantic. The pilots discovered it to be the American " Dixie Clipper," on the Azores-Lisbon run. Feeling the need to relax, they crept up on it from astern, dived under it, and pulling up in front of the pilot's cockpit performed a series of slow rolls for the edification of the passengers. That this was reprehensible must be admitted, and unfortunately during the exhibition one of the Martlets' machine-guns went off. The effect on the Clipper was electric. The pilot fired a red Very light to warn the Martlets off, and an old lady was seen at one of the cabin windows violently waving a pair of white bloomers, which were torn out of her hand by the slipstream and wound themselves round the wing of a Martlet. The pilots returned to the carrier with their first trophy.

The remainder of the voyage was uneventful, although on the return passage (with another large convoy) the Martlets sometimes had to land on when the rise and fall of the flight-deck was 65 feet, as measured by sextant, and the ship was rolling 16 degrees. One skidded over the side and was lost, but the pilot was rescued.

During the Audacity's second voyage, in November, the Commanding Officer of the squadron, Lieutenant-Commander J. M. Wintour, R.N., damaged a prowling Focke-Wulf, but was himself shot down and killed, a cannon shell passing straight through his aircraft. The second pilot, Sub-Lieutenant (A) D. A. Hutchison, R.N., took over the attack and finished off the Focke-Wulf, which was then in flames.

On the afternoon of the same day there was another alarm. By that time there was only one serviceable aircraft in the ship and one with a bent airscrew. Sub-Lieutenant (A) E. M. Brown, R.N.V.R., volunteered to fly the latter, and the two Martlets went up. While climbing they became separated in cloud. Sub-Lieutenant Brown intercepted two Focke-Wulfs approaching in formation. He made four attacks on one of them before it escaped into the cloud below, then followed it down and finished it off in a head-on attack. It spun into the sea from 10,000 feet, and the port wing broke off as it reached the water. The convoy reached Gibraltar without loss.

On the first night of the return passage the homeward-bound convoy was shadowed by two Focke-Wulfs, and a lurking U-boat sank a straggling tanker. In five days the Martlet pilots sighted no less than 17 U-boats on the surface and directed the destroyers on to them. Three were definitely destroyed, one being rammed by H.M.S. Stork.

One morning, when the whole squadron was in the air, it intercepted three Focke-Wulfs. Sub-Lieutenant Brown destroyed one ; the other two were damaged and sheered off. In the afternoon Lieutenant J. W. Sleigh, R.N., and Sub-Lieutenant (A) H. E. Williams, R.N.V.R., accounted for another. During this combat Lieutenant Sleigh collided with the Focke-Wulf and returned with one of its wings dangling from his Martlet's tail.

That day the Martlets put in a total of 30 hours' flying. The last two had to land on in the dark, when the ship was rolling 14 degrees. Neither pilot had made a night landing before.

An hour later a torpedo struck the ship on the port beam, below the mess decks. She went down by the stern until the gun platform was awash. The engines were stopped, but Commander McKendrick would not abandon her, hoping to get her in tow. Twenty minutes later a second torpedo hit her, this time on the port bow, and three more within five minutes. The bow structure collapsed and she reared her stern almost vertically into the air. The aircraft broke adrift on the flight-deck, wrecking the lifeboats and dinghies which had not already been destroyed. The submarine was plainly visible 200 yards away on the port beam, and as the ship went down the Audacity's gunners engaged her with their Oerlikons. Corvettes picked up the survivors, but the losses were heavy, including the Commanding Officer and two of the pilots.

The ship sank within a few miles of the scene of her pilots' first combat. During her brief career as a carrier her aircraft had destroyed five Focke-Wulfs and damaged three, and had contributed to the sinking of three submarines and the scuttling of a fourth. Such is the record of the Audacity.

12.   ROOF OVER THE CONVOY

CARRIERS have been escorting merchant shipping since the beginning of the war. In December, 1939, H.M.S. Furious escorted the first great convoy carrying Canadian troops to Great Britain. She was the flagship, and although it was an anxious passage, with 500 miles through thick white fog and the pocket-battleship Deutschland at large, she brought the convoy safely through.

The Eagle escorted the first Australian convoy to Aden, and at one time or another during the war every aircraft carrier in the Fleet has been employed on trade protection, usually in company with at least one capital ship. The combination of battleship, cruiser and carrier, with a destroyer screen, makes an ideal covering force. The carrier can send her reconnaissance aircraft into the sky to give warning of hostile movement or to detect submarines, while her fighters inter-

cept shadowers and attack enemy formations ; the destroyers hunt the submarines which the aircraft have sighted, the cruiser can make contact with surface vessels, and the big guns of the battleship can deal with a sortie by the enemy fleet, or put a barrage over the Force and the convoy.

For many months the Ark Royal operated in this way in the Eastern Atlantic or the Western Mediterranean while in company with Force H, and at the same time the Eagle, and later the Illustrious and the Formidable, were working with the Mediterranean Fleet. The carriers did even more than give protection from the air, for, as part of a convoy themselves, they have ferried over 800 R.A.F. aircraft to places overseas, including Norway and Malta.

In no part of the world have convoys met with opposition so fierce as on the

TO THE RELIEF OF MALTA. The great east-bound convoy of August, 1942, is passing into the Mediterranean. In the foreground is the carrier Furious. Beyond her ships of the convoy steam steadily on.

E. N. Syfret, flying his flag in H.M.S. Nelson, commanded the covering force (Force F). Rear-Admiral H. M. Burrough, C.B., was in command of the escort.

Day One passed quietly. There was a hot sun in a clear blue sky as the convoy steamed steadily to the eastward. The fighters were ranged in readiness on the flight-decks. The crews of the Albacores had been told off to the ships' guns. It was a new role for them. The fighter pilots begged them to confine their attentions to hostile aircraft.

By next morning the convoy had come within range of the enemy snoopers. A fighter patrol flew off at first light and a standing force of four was kept over the convoy throughout the day.

Halfway through the forenoon a shadower was detected : the first certain intimation that the convoy had been sighted. Fighters from the Indomitable drove it off with one engine on fire, shakily losing height.

As the morning wore on, several more shadowers appeared. Carriers follow the sound naval custom of telling the ship's company below decks what is happening in an operation. From time to time the loud-speakers sounded.

" D'ye hear there ! A small group of aircraft, presumed hostile, is approaching the convoy from the north-east. Our fighters have been sent to intercept."

As yet there had been no air attack. But at sea there are dangers other than from the air. At 1.16 a series of explosions shook the Victorious and Indomitable.

" God ! " said someone. " Eagle ! Look at the Eagle ! "

Smoke was pouring from her. The great flight-deck was already listing to port. Her sister ships increased speed, zig-zagging violently as they took avoiding action. A

passage to Malta. As that opposition increased it became necessary to strengthen the convoys' protection from the air. This was possible only by employment of more than one carrier to deal with the weight of the air attack, and on 9th August, 1942, three carriers passed through the Straits of Gibraltar to escort a great convoy of merchantmen for the relief of Malta : the Victorious (Captain H. C. Bovell, C.B.E., R.N.), wearing the flag of Rear-Admiral A. L. St. G. Lyster, the Indomitable (Captain T. H. Troubridge, R.N.) and the Eagle (Captain L. D. Mackintosh, D.S.C., R.N.). The carriers had a combined strength of some seventy fighters, including Sea-Hurricanes, Martlets and Fulmars. The Furious, which was ferrying aircraft for Malta, was part of the convoy. The Argus remained at Gibraltar with replacements. Vice-Admiral pandemonium of underwater explosions broke out. The loudspeakers spoke again :

" The Eagle has been hit by a number of torpedoes fired by a submarine and she is sinking. The explosions you can hear are depth-charge attacks being made by the destroyers. The air raid that was approaching the convoy has been turned away by our fighters and at least one enemy aircraft has been shot down."

The Eagle sank within ten minutes of being struck. Sixty-seven officers, including Captain Mackintosh, and 862 ratings were saved. Many of her aircraft sank with her. Those of her pilots who were in the air at the time of the attack landed on the Victorious and the Indomitable.

One of these pilots, who had made an emergency landing signal, circled the ship until his companions and the returning patrol from the Victorious had landed. His windscreen was covered with oil and his petrol was almost exhausted, but fearing that he might crash on landing he waited, lest by encumbering the deck he should prevent others from following him until the wreckage had been cleared away.

A few minutes after the Eagle had gone a torpedo track crossed the bow of the Victorious. No less than six U-boats were sighted during the afternoon. The ships continued on their zig-zag course. The destroyers dropped more depth charges. The Furious flew off her Spitfires for Malta and returned to Gibraltar, her mission fulfilled.

For a while there was an ominous lull. The dog watches dragged on and only small

THREE CARRIERS TO PROTECT THEM. The August convoy for Malta is guarded by (left to right) the Indomitable, the Victorious and the Eagle. Between them they carry some 70 fighters. Hurricanes, Martlets and Fulmars.

ON THE FLIGHT DECK THEY WAIT.
Everything is ready. It is 9th August, the first day
of the convoy's passage, and all is still quiet. The
sun shines brightly, and the blue sky is clear. The
convoy is not yet within the range of enemy bombers.

groups of enemy aircraft approached. They
did not wait to fight and were driven off.
Dusk darkened sea and sky. The carriers
waited for the attack they knew must come.

The scene in the Victorious may be
described by one of the officers on board :

" The stand-by squadron was all set on
deck, the pilots in their cockpits gazing up-
wards and perhaps munching a biscuit.
Men stood by the lanyards which secured
the wing-tips ; men lay by their chocks ;
men sat astride their starter motors. The
deck officers fiddled with their flags and
Commander Flying nursed his flight-deck
microphone. They were all waiting :
waiting for those vital 17 seconds which
would follow the Boatswain's Mate's call
' Fighters stand-to.' The eighteenth second

THE BATTLE RAGES. On the evening of the 10th August the bombers come. In the twilight of that day and all next day the battle is fought out between the enemy bombers and the Fleet's fighters and guns. Here the sky is filled with shell bursts, as the merchant ships plod on.

should see the ship returning to her station and the fighters airborne over the sea."

Suddenly the call came. The Fulmar squadron flew off and merged into the gathering darkness. The Indomitable's Hurricanes were already engaging the raiders—35 Ju. 88s. Some they drove off, but the failing light made combat difficult. Two of the bandits broke through.

" Salvoes ! Salvoes ! " went the warning signal for the fighters to haul off and keep clear of the guns coming into action. The carriers' 4.5s, the multiple pom-poms and the Oerlikons, poured a barrage into the twilight sky as the great ships twisted and turned to avoid the bombs. Two fell close to the Victorious ; the bombers which dropped them, silhouetted against the sunset, fell to the guns of the ship. One crashed blazing into the sea " like a torch of fire in a sheaf". The remainder dropped their bombs in desperation to escape the fighters waiting for them outside the barrage.

When the attack was over there was haste to land on the fighters which had been longest in the sky. A Hurricane from the Indomitable, out of petrol, had to land on the Victorious while the ship was still out of wind and under wheel. Coming on while the flight-deck was still slewing to starboard, it hit another aircraft stowed abaft the island and burst into flames. The pilot escaped unhurt. Led by the Air Technical Officer a party dashed in to extract the un-expended ammunition before it exploded, while one of the Albacore pilots from a nearby Oerlikon played a hose on them all. The crash was cleared within six minutes, freeing the flight-deck for the remaining fighters to scramble on.

Six were found to be missing from the Victorious. The ship turned back upon her course to rejoin the convoy. At length tiny blue lights signalled from the In-domitable that the missing aircraft were safe. One of the pilots is said to have sat spinning yarns for 20 minutes before he discovered that he was not in his own ship.

That was the end of Day Two. No ship in the convoy had been damaged. The night that followed was one of vigilance for those on deck, and in the crowded hangars and workshops one of preparation for the morrow, as the maintenance ratings sweated and strained to get every possible aircraft fit for service by daylight. One Hurricane had to have a complete tail unit and its airscrew changed, and a serious leak in the hydraulic system repaired : work which might have taken 48 hours in a yard ashore.

Day Three was to be the test of endurance, as all knew, with the coast of Africa but 50 miles to the south, and the convoy within range of the airfields in Sardinia and Sicily. Now enemy fighters could accompany the bombing formations, and more determined raids were to be expected.

An Italian S. 79 shadower was the Fulmars' first victim of the day. It dived in a flaming spiral to hit the sea within half a mile of the North African shore. At 9 o'clock, as reinforcements went up from the Victorious to augment the standing patrol, the leader saw the Indomitable's Hurricanes diving on a formation of twenty Ju. 88s. Two of the bombers went into the sea like stones. Ten jettisoned their bombs. The Hurricanes from the Victorious caught two more as they swept past. In less than two minutes the sky was clear. The convoy steamed on, untouched.

So the day passed. As the enemy forma-tions came over, hour after hour, Hurricanes, Martlets and Fulmars shot up into the sky, forcing them to drop wide or shooting them down. One pilot said he found it hard to decide whether the crews were baling out before or after he had pressed the button. One large formation of Cant. Z 1007 torpedo-carriers could do no more than " circle round at a distance, like hyenas " ; the fighters did not let one come within five miles of the convoy.

" Then," wrote the officer in the Vic-torious, " two Reggiane fighters dived down on our port quarter, levelled off two miles away and came roaring over the flight-deck, just a few feet up. Everyone thought they were Hurries, pleased with themselves, and someone remarked, ' How they like to play ! ' But no, they were Reggianes, and as they came they bounced a couple of ' cricket balls ' along the flight-deck and disappeared in a trail of white smoke. One ' cricket ball ' was a dud and broke up without exploding. The other burst in the water alongside, breaking the anti-submarine look-out's bin-oculars."

During the afternoon there was a lull but, as Captain Bovell wrote in his report, " frequent submarine alarms kept interest alive." A U-boat was brought to the surface by depth-charges. The destroyers rammed and sank her.

" Soon after 1700," continued Captain Bovell, " the air woke up again ard between

ORDEAL. You would think no ship could live through this. But she reached Malta, while above her and her sister ships the Navy's fighters destroyed at least 39 enemy bombers for a loss of eight: their greatest victory.

1730 and 1900 every available fighter was operating continuously, engaging shadowers and intercepting groups of incoming raiders. About 1815 large groups were detected and every fighter was at once put in the air. These groups when intercepted were found to consist of Ju. 88s, Cant. Z. 1007s, S. 79s, Me. 110s, Me. 109s and Me. 202s. Though at a serious disadvantage, all our fighters engaged the enemy, shooting down and damaging many, and generally breaking up the groups."

One formation of twenty bombers, however, broke through and dived on to the Indomitable. She was damaged by a near miss, but although she continued under her own steam she could not operate her aircraft, and those which were in the air landed on the Victorious. One of these pilots, Sub-Lieutenant M. Hankey, though advised to rest, insisted on going into the sky again.

As soon as his Hurricane had been refuelled he flew off, shot down an enemy aircraft, and was last seen with another on his tail.

By 7.30 the enemy had broken off the attack. Rear-Admiral Burrough's flagship, the cruiser Nigeria, sustained temporary damage, but half an hour later she was on an even keel. The convoy was still intact and only 130 miles from Malta. Beaufighters of the R.A.F. took over the patrol and by daylight there would be Spitfires. The two carriers turned towards the setting sun, their task accomplished. As the Indomitable approached Gibraltar, the Royal Marines played their wounded ship into harbour, making a gesture of defiance by using as their bandstand the top of her buckled for'ard lift.

It had been the naval fighters' greatest battle, and greatest victory. Some 70 fighters, only one of them armed with cannon, had been opposed to a force of at least 500 bombers, torpedo-aircraft and fighter escorts. Yet in spite of the losses of the aircraft in the *Eagle*, in spite of being outnumbered, out-distanced and out-gunned, the Martlets, Hurricanes and Fulmars had shot down 39 enemy aircraft and nine probables, damaging more, for the loss of only eight of their own. One pilot alone, Lieutenant R. J. Cork, D.S.C., R.N., who took over one of the *Indomitable's* squadrons when his leader, Lieutenant-Commander F. E. C. Judd, D.S.C., R.N., had been brought down, accounted for three Germans, three Italians, and one probable, a German. Even more important than the number of enemy aircraft destroyed, the convoy and the escorting forces had been protected, thanks to the courage, skill and grim determination of the fighter pilots, 90 per cent of whom belonged to the Royal Naval Volunteer Reserve.

Writing of their magnificent work, Vice-Admiral Syfret declared : " Flying at great heights, constantly chasing the faster Ju. 88s, warning the Fleet of approaching formations, breaking up the latter, and in the later stages doing their work in the face of superior enemy fighter forces—they were grand."

Nor must the work of those who kept the fighters in the sky be forgotten. The flight-deck parties, composed of Able Seamen, had been on duty from dawn till dusk ranging the aircraft, placing the chocks in position and removing them on the signal, releasing the landing aircraft's hooks from the arrester wires, and folding the wings. On Day Three the party in the *Victorious* made 86 journeys up and down the flight-deck, a distance of something like 20 miles. In the hangars " the maintenance ratings worked like slaves in the cramped space. The floors were covered with grease and running with oil and petrol. The heat was intense and they had to work all the time under electric light, taking their food in the hangars as and when they could." That is the tribute of a pilot in the *Victorious* to those in whose devoted service the fighters did not trust in vain.

The operational problem of convoying merchant ships to Malta is not dissimilar from that of convoying them to Murmansk or Archangel. As in the Mediterranean, the route through the Barents Sea lies within reach of the enemy heavy bombers but beyond the range of British shore-based fighters, so that once again the only means of giving effective air cover is by carrier. The passage of the Malta convoys had shown that it was possible to give fighter protection from carriers in the Mediterranean. In September, 1942, similar protection was given in the Arctic to the largest and most valuable convoy ever sent to Russia up to that time.

The composition of the two escort forces was, however, very different, and only a single carrier was employed. The escort force was commanded by Rear-Admiral R. L. Burnett, O.B.E., with his flag in the cruiser *Scylla*. Rear-Admiral E. K. Boddam-

HAVEN. The convoy gets through. In the Grand Harbour, Malta, the supplies are unloaded throughout the night in the glare of arc lamps

FIGHTING THROUGH TO RUSSIA. The largest convoy that had so far been assembled for Russia set sail in September, 1942. Flying low over the Barents Sea, on 14th September, these seven Junkers 88s are part of a large force singling out the convoy's aircraft-carrier for attack. They were met by fighters and gunfire, and the attack failed.

Whetham, D.S.O., was Commodore of the convoy. He was the first officer of the rank of Commander to qualify as an observer in the Fleet Air Arm after the last war.

Before the convoy sailed it was known that the Luftwaffe had strengthened the Fifth Air Fleet, based on Norway, by the transfer of Heinkel 111s (which carry two torpedoes), Ju. 88 dive-bombers, Focke-Wulf Kuriers, and Me. 109F fighters. This gave an operational strength of 300 bombers alone.

Shadowers and U-boats sighted the convoy on 9th September, but the enemy attack did not begin until the 12th, when the ships were to the northward of Narvik. The Hurricanes shot down a Heinkel 111, but unfortunately they expended their energy in chasing the heavily-armoured Bloem and Voss 138 shadowers under cloud conditions,

so that when the main attack came they were unprepared, and a formation of 37 torpedo-aircraft broke through and sank several ships in the convoy.

Next day the Hurricane pilots profited by that experience, conserved their strength, and concentrated their power. The enemy tried to throw the escort and convoy into confusion by dropping mines from aircraft and by high level bombing attacks before sending in the torpedo-carriers. The Heinkels swept into action in line abreast, flying in close formation only a few feet above the sea, fanning out as they approached. High above the Junkers and Heinkels flew a fighter escort of Messerschmitts.

" You could see them coming in layers, like a wedding cake," said one of the carrier's

THE CONVOY GOES THROUGH.   Thanks to the barrage and the carrier's Hurricanes, the convoy arrived in Russia with no warships sunk and relatively fewer merchant ship losses than in any previous convoy.

pilots, " and as we took off, it looked as though we had about three aircraft to every layer of Jerries. Our squadrons had to split up to tackle various bunches of Huns, and eventually I found myself with my section mate—a Petty Officer, who was a wizard pilot and a grand fighter—tackling 14 Junkers 88s flying in diamond formation, a pretty hard nut to crack, for if they can keep formation, their cross fire keeps every plane covered.

" However, I made a quarter attack on the leading plane, then swung away straight at one of the planes on the side of the diamond. At the last second I flicked underneath him ; he got the wind up and pulled the nose of his plane hard up, and the Petty Officer, flying just on my starboard wing, gave him a lovely burst which put paid to his account. The formation broke up, and there was a lovely scrap all over the sky.

" That sort of thing went on all day. As soon as we were out of ammunition or petrol, we dived down to the carrier, landed, re-armed and re-fuelled and took off again. My lunch was a gulp of cold tea. Our squadron made 17 sorties that day.

" I saw two Heinkels, having launched their torpedoes, flying along the side of the carrier dead level with the bridge. The gunners waited till they were only a few yards away, opened up—and the sky and sea were full of bits of Heinkel, an amazing sight."

During the afternoon of the 14th the enemy decided to strike at the root of the fighter opposition by attacking the carrier with a force of Heinkels and Junkers which aimed 17 torpedoes at her and a shower of bombs. But the fighters attacked the Heinkels and spoilt their aim. The Commanding Officer, who had had considerable experience as a torpedo pilot, handled his ship so superbly that she came through unscathed. Later she made a signal to the flagship that she had " the honour of being the sole object of the attack " and claimed four enemy aircraft destroyed and three probables.

Next day the enemy abandoned torpedo attacks, but kept up high and low level bombing on the escort and convoy for three hours. No warships were sunk during the passage and although the ranks of the merchantmen were thinned, they had come through with relatively fewer losses than any previous convoy, thanks not only to the terrific barrage the whole force was able to produce, accounting for 35 German aircraft, but also to the carrier's Hurricanes.

" I shall never forget the reckless gallantry of the naval pilots in their determination to get in among the enemy despite the solid mass of our defence fire," wrote Rear-Admiral Burnett.

They destroyed five German aircraft, with three probables, and damaged 14 for the loss of four Hurricanes, three of whose pilots were saved. Throughout the passage the Swordfish had carried out anti-submarine patrols, sometimes flying in icing conditions at 500 feet. They sighted a number of U-boats, kept them down with depth-charges and guided the destroyers to them ; at least once this co-operation led to a kill.

The carrier returned with Rear-Admiral Burnett's escort force and a homeward-bound convoy. Before sailing the Commanding Officer spared no effort to render every aircraft in the ship fit to fly again. Rear-Admiral Burnett made a signal congratulating him on being such a good father to his children. " The nursery door is now definitely closed " was the reply. So decisive had been the victory over the Luftwaffe, however, that on the return passage there were no attacks from the air.

It is fitting to end this chapter with David's words after he had been delivered out of the hand of Saul :

" I have pursued mine enemies, and destroyed them ; and turned not again until I had consumed them. And I have consumed and wounded them, that they could not arise ; yea they have fallen under my feet."

Such was the Fleet Air Arm's answer to those who said that carriers cannot operate within range of enemy shore-based aircraft.

WHEN

THE SERVICES COMBINE

ALTHOUGH the most spectacular achievements of the Fleet Air Arm have been those of carrier-borne aircraft, nevertheless the squadrons based ashore have been doing essential work since the early days of the war. Among them are the second-line squadrons which assist in the training of pilots, observers and air-gunners, and the Fleet Requirements Units which tow targets, act as spotters for practice gunfire, fly at varying heights to exercise the gunners of the capital ships in range-finding, and make mock attacks on the Fleet.

There are also Communication Squadrons at Lee and Donibristle which fly in all weathers to anywhere in the British Isles with passengers, mails and freight. The squadron at Donibristle was formed after the German occupation of the Channel Islands, when the pilots of the Jersey Airways Company brought all their aircraft away, with 35 engineers and their families, and offered themselves as a body to the Admiralty. The pilots were given commissions in the R.N.V.R. ; the engineers remained civilians but stayed with their aircraft. The squadron has been considerably enlarged and since 1st July, 1940, has flown over $1\frac{1}{2}$ million miles, carrying 40,000 passengers and 1,300 tons of freight.

First-line shore-based squadrons have performed an immense amount of valuable and largely unrecorded service while operating with the R.A.F. from Coastal and Bomber Commands stations in Great Britain, and from Malta, Gibraltar, Greece, Crete, the Western Desert, and other more distant points.

During April, 1940, a squadron of Swordfish was employed under Coastal Command for minelaying operations. A month later the invasion of the Low Countries called for urgent air reinforcements, and by the end of May two squadrons of Skuas, four of Swordfish and one of Albacores (the first to be used operationally) had been lent to Coastal Command. The period of their attachment varied from a few days to ten months. They patrolled over the Channel, carried out coastal photographic reconnaissance, dive-bombed roads and bridges and other military objectives such as enemy tanks, guns, ammunition dumps, motor transport, shipping, barges and E-boats. Often they operated by night, raiding enemy ports, airfields, oil installations and power stations, or dropped mines in German, Dutch and Belgian waterways. Sometimes they worked independently, at others in co-operation with R.A.F. squadrons, or with an escort of R.A.F. fighters.

Much of the work was new to the naval air crews. Their aircraft were not designed for daylight raids over enemy territory, and many of their tasks were remote from the Fleet work for which they had been trained. Often they had to face intense opposition from enemy fighters and anti-aircraft defences.

During the Dunkirk evacuation they continued their activities, protecting convoys, attacking concentrations of troops and barges, and bombing gun positions. One squadron of 12 Swordfish was set on by a swarm of Me. 109s and only five returned. After the capitulation of France they turned their attention to the invasion ports, spotted for the warship bombardments of French and Belgian harbours, shared in the R.A.F. raids on Brest and Lorient, and continued their convoy duties and security patrols. The Rocs, two-seater fighter-dive-bombers, which had but a short operational history, also took part in the raids with the Skuas, once attacking E-boats at Boulogne.

Some 40 T.B.R. pilots also served with R.A.F. bomber squadrons during the Battle of Britain (the fighter pilots have already been mentioned), flying Whitleys and Wellingtons with R.A.F. crews. One of them made over 30 trips before being shot down over Berlin.

Early in August a squadron of Walrus aircraft, drawn from ships of the Home Fleet, was disembarked to the Shetlands, where it operated for many months under Coastal Command, carrying out anti-submarine patrols in the adverse conditions which another Walrus squadron had been facing in Iceland.

The minelaying by the T.B.R. aircraft was particularly valuable. This is an exacting duty which requires unobtrusive action and accurate navigation by night. It has none of the excitement of a bombing raid or a torpedo attack, and those engaged in it seldom have the satisfaction of observing the results. To ensure secrecy, the aircraft usually fly independently, but occasionally a striking force has been used to create a diversion by dropping bombs, particularly in the Mediterranean, for minelaying by naval aircraft has not been confined to home waters. The long distances to be covered entailed fitting the aircraft with overload petrol tanks, which nestled behind the pilot's back on the one hand and the observer's neck on the other. The air-gunner had to be left behind, and the observer, besides handling the after gun, had to work out his navigation and operate his wireless in acute discomfort. It is said that one officer had to buy an abdominal belt before he could change the frequency of his transmitter.

This co-operation with Coastal and Bomber Commands still continues. At R.A.F. stations on the east and south coasts so-called " lodger units " of the Fleet Air Arm are doing useful work, minelaying, patrolling, and seeking out enemy vessels to destroy. The relations between the two Services are excellent, and although the R.A.F. may chaff the naval airmen about their antiquated Stringbags, they recognise the value of the work they do and are quick to avenge their losses. On one occasion, after a minelaying

Swordfish had been shot down, the R.A.F. pilots of the station obtained permission to raid the hangars of the airfield from which the enemy fighters had come, and made a successful job of it.

Equally happy has been the co-operation at Malta, where naval aircraft have been working under R.A.F. control since Italy entered the war. In May, 1940, a training squadron of 24 Swordfish was based at Hyères, in the south of France. Twelve Swordfish were formed into a striking force to operate under the French Admiralty should Mussolini decide to fight. That decision was made on 10th June, and on the 14th nine Swordfish, manned by instructors and pupils and led by Lieutenant-Commander G. C. Dickins, R.N., had the satisfaction of being the first aircraft to drop bombs on Italian soil. They were French bombs, secured with spun yarn and fused before taking off. Twenty-three of them landed on Genoa, with unknown results.

At 2 a.m. on the 17th, the squadron received a signal from London to leave France. The French authorities put no obstacles in the way, and next morning the 24 Swordfish, in two formations, took off for the French naval air station at Bône on the Algerian coast, carrying some of the maintenance ratings with them. The distance was 430 miles and the flight took them four hours and twenty minutes : near the limit of their endurance, for they had no reserve tanks. The French airmen treated them well ; all the French officers wanted to go on fighting.

At Bône the squadron split up. The training half returned to England, via Casablanca and Gibraltar. The striking force, under Lieutenant-Commander F. D. Howie, R.N., flew via Medjez-el-Bab to Malta, where they began operations under the R.A.F. against targets in Sicily. They made a night bombing raid on the oil tanks at Augusta, and bombed Catania airfield, scoring a direct hit on one of the hangars. Once they made a search for a force of fifteen destroyers and cruisers which had been reported ; it proved to be

OFF TO STRIKE FROM MALTA. Naval ratings unfold the wings of an Albacore standing in its pen at an R.A.F. Station in Malta. The pen gives protection against the blast from enemy bombs.

the shadows of fifteen small clouds. On another occasion the Squadron Commander noted in his flying log : " Brilliant dawn attack on wreck."

During this period two Swordfish were always standing by at 15 minutes' readiness for anti-submarine duty, and the squadron worked up for its proper function—torpedo attacks. They began with a daylight attack on a convoy, which was shadowed by a Sunderland flying-boat. Three ships were intercepted, one was sunk, another damaged. Dusk attacks followed, one flight being armed with torpedoes and two with bombs.

During the winter the squadron made bombing raids on Palermo and Tripoli, and laid mines in North African harbours, the Wellingtons sometimes providing diversion with high-level bombing attacks. And all the time the remorseless striking of the Italian convoys sailing from Sicily to Tripoli and Benghazi went on. The convoys, consisting of half a dozen merchant ships and an escort of destroyers, would sail in the morning. An R.A.F. aircraft on reconnaissance between Sicily and Cape Bon would sight one, return, and then pick it up again at dusk. The naval striking force would time its departure from Malta to arrive over the convoy in the dark. Its main difficulty was to elude the standing

patrol of Messerschmitts which encircled the island by day, waiting to intercept a striking force as it returned after dawn.

Some of the Swordfish were 1935 types, with no blind-flying instruments. Their losses were remarkably small in comparison with the number of sorties they made, but the maintenance party, who were exposed to incessant danger on the ground, had difficulty in keeping them serviceable during the long succession of heavy raids. The landing-ground sometimes received more than 100 bombs in a day, and was what one of the pilots described as " decidedly bumpy." In addition to the daylight raids, the Germans tried to stop the Swordfish from leaving the ground by keeping at least one aircraft over the airfield all night, dropping bombs at short intervals. " This practice," wrote the same pilot, " made it very uncomfortable while taxi-ing to the take-off position, and sometimes entailed taking off without knowing whether bomb splinters or shrapnel had penetrated any vital part of the aircraft." Even delayed-action bombs on the runways of the airfield, however, did not prevent the Swordfish from going into the sky when a convoy was reported, sometimes twice in a night.

Often these raids would be made in co-operation with the R.A.F. On 22nd July, 1941, Blenheim bombers found a convoy of four large Italian merchant ships off Pantellaria, and hit three of them. One blew up, another sank. Later in the day the naval striking force attacked the two remaining vessels with torpedoes, sinking a large tanker and hitting one of the escorting destroyers. A few nights later the Fleet Air Arm reversed the procedure by sinking two vessels of a convoy of six off the island of Lampedusa, leaving the Blenheims to tackle the remainder next morning.

Once the Malta squadrons shared the honours with an Albacore squadron based in Libya. Both had the same objective—a convoy of four liner troopships carrying reinforcements to Tripoli, escorted by an

Italian battleship, four cruisers and at least fifteen destroyers. R.A.F. reconnaissance sighted this formidable force steaming to the southward on the afternoon of 23rd January, 1942. A striking force of nine Albacores and Swordfish left Malta soon after 8 p.m. that evening. The weather was terrible : heavy rainstorms and a strong north-easterly wind. There was no hope of it improving ; there had been a *gregale* warning at Malta. Seven of the Swordfish were compelled to turn back for one reason or another ; some returned after three hours' constant battering by the storm. The leader, Lieutenant-Commander F. H. E. Hopkins, D.S.C., R.N., and one other pilot drove on and on, determined to find the enemy. After flying 80 miles past the position in which they had expected to sight the convoy they found it at last. By that time they were well over their safety limit of petrol, and since it would take them half an hour to deliver an attack from where they were, they decided to return to Malta and collect another striking force.

They battled their way back, and Lieutenant-Commander Hopkins, in spite of the increasing storm, organized a second striking force of six aircraft, which he led himself. They took off at 2.45 a.m. Two failed to keep formation and were forced to return, but the remainder found the convoy again at 5.45 and obtained two hits on the 24,000-ton Lloyd-Triestino liner *Victoria*. They landed after 6½ hours' flying : their permitted endurance was 5½ hours.

The initiative and determination of Lieutenant-Commander Hopkins had been magnificent, and he had flown for 11 hours 50 minutes in conditions which normally would have been considered impossible. He received the immediate award of the D.S.O.

Meanwhile five Albacores from a squadron which was operating with the R.A.F. from a captured landing-ground near Benghazi had taken off to find the same target, flying through the same storm. Towards sunset they sighted the convoy at long range. One of the pilots aimed his torpedo at an escorting destroyer, causing a violent explosion. The leader, Lieutenant-Commander J. W. S. Corbett, D.S.O., R.N., with great gallantry singled out the battleship, but his aircraft was shot down, and no results were claimed for his attack. He and his crew were picked up by an Italian hospital ship and taken prisoner. Lieutenant (A) H. M. Ellis, R.N., eluding two Ju. 88s, which were escorting the convoy, dropped his torpedo at the *Victoria*, striking her under the for'ard funnel. She sank later, under the combined attack.

Lieutenant Ellis's aircraft was hit by one of the destroyers, and was also attacked by the Ju. 88s, but he succeeded in reaching his base after a flight of 150 miles across the sea. He was awarded the D.F.C., and since he was subsequently awarded the D.S.C. he had the unusual distinction of winning both naval and R.A.F. decorations.

The naval air squadrons at Malta received much help and encouragement from Air Vice-Marshal H. P. Lloyd, when he was Air Officer Commanding ; he always referred to the Swordfish as his " goldfish ", and for every ship they sank he presented the squadron with a bottle of rare and precious Plymouth gin.

By the end of 1942 naval air squadrons at Malta had accounted for something like 400,000 tons of enemy merchant shipping. While naval aircraft were attacking enemy convoys in the Central Mediterranean another squadron, operating under the R.A.F. from Gibraltar, was protecting British and Allied shipping by watching for U-boats in the Straits. Four Swordfish and eight crews were on duty every night, each crew patrolling for two hours. Depth-charges had replaced bombs as weapons of attack, and during one period of three weeks alone the squadron accounted for two submarines destroyed and four probables ; often the destroyers carried on the work which the Swordfish had begun.

Farther east, in February, 1941, a squadron of T.B.R. aircraft from the damaged *Illustrious* was transferred to the naval air station at Maleme in Crete, under Lieu-tenant-Commander J. de F. Jago, R.N., with the object of preventing the Italian fleet from penetrating into the Ægean. In the following month a composite squadron of Fulmars and Brewster Buffaloes under Lieutenant-Commander Alan Black, D.S.C., R.N., arrived from Egypt to provide fighter protection for the Swordfish, the naval base at Suda Bay and the convoys, and in general to combat the increasing force of the enemy air attacks. The squadron's first loss was when three Fulmars took off to intercept a large formation of Italian S.79s escorted by C.R. 42s. The Fulmars ran into thick clouds and only one of them, piloted by Sub-Lieutenant (A.) R. C. Kay, R.N.V.R., with Leading Airman Stockman as his air-gunner, succeeded in engaging the enemy bombers. They shot down one, damaged two and collided with a fourth, before they met their end. It was their first combat.

At the beginning of March, when the Italians were making their second thrust into Epirus and sending supplies and rein-forcements from Brindisi to the Albanian ports of Valona and Durazzo, the greater part of the Swordfish squadron moved to Greece, operating from Eleusis, near Athens. The R.A.F. lent the squadron a technical officer, and the Royal Hellenic Navy put the whole of the torpedo depot at its dis-posal. On the day after arrival the squad-1on moved to an advanced base at Para-mythia, at the head of a valley in the Albanian mountains, from which the R.A.F. had been operating against the Italian lines of com-munication. There was a rough natural landing-ground, with good camouflage. Snow was still lying on the hills, but the valley was clear, although bitterly cold. The R.A.F. gave the squadron officers sleeping quarters, allowed them to use their galleys and transport, and lent them main-tenance personnel.

The task of the Swordfish was to work round the coast opposite Corfu and to attack shipping in Valona harbour. Lieu-tenant-Commander Jago and Lieutenant J. A. Caldecott-Smith, R.N., the senior observer, were missing after the first raid, and Lieutenant F. M. A. Torrens-Spence, R.N., took over command. The squadron made five attacks during the March moon period. The Italians took to sending the convoys to Durazzo, whither the Swordfish followed them, claiming three hits in a single night. By the next moon period the German attack had begun. The Jugoslavs were reported (incorrectly) to have captured Durazzo, so the squadron attacked Brindisi, the Italian end of the convoy route, laying mines and torpedoing a tanker in the inner harbour.

The last raid was made on 1st April, when Lieutenant Torrens-Spence torpedoed an ammunition ship in Valona harbour. Then the German advance forced the squadron to move back to Eleusis, and finally to evacuate, the last two Swordfish flying off to Maleme as the Messerschmitts came in to attack.

The squadron had good reason to feel satisfied with the five weeks' work, for it had sunk five Italian ships and damaged five more, and these raids, made after long night flights over mountainous country, often in bad weather, had played no small part in the success of the Greek Army in Albania.

At the beginning of May the naval air station at Maleme was handed over to the R.A.F., but remained under the direction of Commander G. H. Beale, R.N., who had been the Air Staff Officer in the *Illustrious*. About 25,000 troops, who had been evacu-ated from Greece, were being organized in Crete. The New Zealanders were sent to defend Maleme airfield. Every effort was made to improve the defences of the station, but the lack of tools and material, and the inadequate supply of labour, made the work very difficult. Since the New Zealanders had not enough Bren guns they rigged up a Browning from a naval aircraft with hand-made mountings.

The story of the naval air operations from Crete during the closing stages of the Allied

THE ILLUSTRIOUS IS ON FIRE, her flight-deck pierced by bombs in a heavy dive-bombing attack. She is west of Malta, escorting a convoy, on 10th January, 1941. The stores, stowed in the roof of the hangar below, are ablaze. The nearly red hot deck is turning the water from the fire hoses into steam. Smoke from the fire below pours through the jagged metal edges of the bomb hole. The after lift has been blown out by bomb hits, and can be seen as a dark shape directly beyond the bomb hole and to the left of the plume of smoke. Six hours later the carrier reached Malta under her own steam.

occupation is a tragic tale of a gallant fight against hopeless odds and impossible conditions. From the outset both the T.B.R. and the fighter aircraft were severely handicapped by inadequate communications and maintenance facilities. Compelled to fly when scarcely serviceable, they had to make repeated forced landings, and as the days went by they had to face increasing enemy activity when in the air, and bombing raids when on the ground. In spite of this, they went time after time into the sky.

At first the attack came from the Italian C.R. 42s, but by the beginning of May Messerschmitts and Junker 88s had taken their place. It became impossible for the Swordfish and the Blenheims to operate, and they returned to Alexandria, leaving the fighters to defend the island from the air.

On 12th May the Luftwaffe began to come over in even greater numbers, the Messerschmitts machine-gunning the defences and the Junkers bombing the station buildings. Three of the Gloster Gladiators which had been added to the fighter squadron were on patrol one morning when they sighted 25 Ju. 88s in line ahead. Two of the Gladiators immediately engaged them, and were never seen again. The third tried to break up a tight formation of six bombers which were circling the airfield. It was last seen losing height over the sea. "Those pilots fought like tigers," said a naval rating who had been watching from the deck of the corvette Salvia in Suda Bay.

These raids increased in severity from day to day and made work on the ground almost impossible. The naval pilots took turns with their R.A.F. comrades in flying the Hurricanes, Fulmars and Gladiators which remained serviceable, sitting ready in the cockpits as they waited for the alarm. Any aircraft which arrived intact from Greece was eagerly pressed into service.

On 16th May three naval pilots, flying Hurricanes, engaged 15 Me.109s which were escorting 30 Ju. 88s. Two pilots were lost, but the third, Lieutenant (A)

WHITE ENSIGN IN CRETE. Shore-based squadrons of the Fleet Air Arm operated in Greece and Crete. Here a sentry stands guard at Maleme Airfield.

A. R. Ramsay, R.N.V.R., shot down two of the enemy. Next day the last Fulmar and the last two Gladiators were destroyed on the ground in a bombing raid, leaving only a single Hurricane fit to fly.

The garrison was expecting eight more Hurricanes with fresh pilots on 20th May (Lieutenant-Commander Black had been sent back to Alexandria to fetch them), but before they could reach the island the airborne invasion began. The opening scene may be described in the words of a naval observer who was present :

"Shortly before dawn on 20th May all the troops stood-to. The sun rose, and everyone was dispersed to wash and breakfast. Then, while the troops were scattered and in different stages of undress, the air raid warning sounded and they took cover in the nearest shelters. Almost immediately wave after wave of enemy fighters and bombers streaked round the airfield, shooting up the camp and paying particular attention to the defence positions all round. The actual landing-ground was left alone.

"For two hours they continued to circle

round at heights from 100-150 feet, gunning and bombing, creating dust, smoke and noise which was frightening in its intensity. Overhead were swarms of troop-carrying aircraft from whose interiors hundreds of parachutists were dropping. Some had already landed, and the air was full of reinforcements as an endless stream of aircraft came and went."

Officers and men rushed to their posts, and Commander Beale ran towards the Battalion Headquarters which was his action station. He was severely wounded by the explosion of a hand-grenade, and subsequently became a prisoner of war. Lieutenant A. W. F. Sutton, D.S.C., R.N., who had been his chief assistant, dashed into his own tent, grabbed his rifle and bandolier, and took up a position on a hill near the 3-inch guns, manned by Royal Marines. Aircraft circled overhead, bombing and machine-gunning any troop movements. Coming under the fire of snipers, he dug himself a hole with his bayonet, and spent the greater part of the day firing at the parachutists who continued to drop in every direction as troop-carrier followed troop-carrier. Strings of gliders, dive-bombers and fighters seemed to fill the sky.

In a pit at the bottom of the hill Leading Aircraftman Denton was manning a Lewis gun. Parachutists were descending all round him, but he kept his gun in action, inflicting a number of casualties, until at length it burnt out and he could fire no more. Picking it up, he scrambled to the defended position at the top of the hill.

As soon as the attack began, the surviving officers and men of the fighter squadron, under the command of Lieutenant Ramsay, had mustered on the high ground overlooking their camp, into which parachutists were falling. Inadequately armed, bombed and machine-gunned from the air, attacked by German infantry and bombarded by a trench-mortar, they held their position for the greater part of the day and killed a number of the enemy. They were short of

supplies, and during the forenoon Chief Petty Officer Hall made his way to the camp through the enemy lines and brought back rum and provisions.

Later in the day the party were joined by Petty Officer Wheaton and a few R.A.F. ranks. This Petty Officer had been attached to the squadron, with two Able Seamen, for electrical work on the airfield. In company with one of the Able Seamen and some R.A.F. ranks he had been driven from trench to trench, fighting back with rifle fire all the time, until surrounded and forced to surrender. Then a German officer gave Wheaton a red flag emblazoned with a black swastika, and ordered him and one of the R.A.F. men to march ahead of a group of Germans armed with Tommy guns. He was directed to shout to any British troops they encountered and call upon them to surrender.

The party advanced, the Petty Officer (flag in hand) and the airman leading. Wheaton whispered to his companion that he intended to make a break for it when the time came. The airman agreed. They approached within ear-shot of a trench manned by New Zealanders with a machine-gun.

" I'm ordered to tell you to surrender," shouted Wheaton, " but I'm going to make a run for your trench."

He dashed forward, the airman beside him. Streams of bullets flew past them in either direction, as both sides opened fire. The airman fell, shot in the back. Wheaton, miraculously, reached the trench unhurt. The Germans were driven back, leaving several dead. The New Zealanders ran out to rescue the airman, who was badly wounded.

Wheaton remained with Lieutenant Ramsay's party, which had to fight its way back next morning, the troops having been forced to retire during the night, and eventually made contact with Lieutenant Sutton in an olive grove to which he and a number of Fleet Air Arm ratings, R.A.F. personnel and soldiers who had lost their units, had retired. There they spent the night of the 21st.

Towards morning the Maoris made a magnificent counter-attack, sweeping into the enemy lines and wiping out one group of Germans after another, until they reached Maleme village. But when daylight broke they could go no farther. Enemy machine-gun posts blocked the way, inflicting heavy losses. Rifles and bayonets were useless against them. The attack slowed down, then halted. The dive-bombers returned, and the enemy received a continued stream of reinforcements from the air. Towards noon on the 22nd the withdrawal began.

Long before dawn the forlorn little party of F.A.A. and R.A.F. officers and men—then about 160 in all—had been re-formed into two groups, the armed and the unarmed. Between them they had 60 rifles and a few revolvers. Their ammunition was almost expended. While the Maoris were counter-attacking they had taken up defensive positions round the camp, but, when the tide turned, Lieutenant Sutton, anxious that the skilled mechanics who composed the majority of his party should not be sacrificed unnecessarily, went to Battalion Headquarters to ask permission to retire. On his way back he met Lieutenant (A) L. K. Keith, R.N., stalking a sniper with a pistol. Before the attack this officer had been down with dysentery, but, determined to do something, and fortified perhaps by the comfortable assurance " as thy day is, so shall thy strength be," he had been spending most of his time in this fantastic and unequal contest.

The New Zealanders' casualties had been so heavy that it was necessary for Lieutenant Sutton's party to guard the flanks of the position that night. Lieutenant Ramsay with the Fleet Air Arm ratings were posted on the right, Lieutenant Sutton and the R.A.F. details took the left.

In the general withdrawal which followed next morning Lieutenant Sutton lost touch with his outposts. It was five days—days of extraordinary experiences and great hard

ships—before he reached Sphakia, on the south coast, when he embarked in H.M.A.S. Napier for Alexandria. Meanwhile the Fleet Air Arm officers and ratings under Lieutenant Ramsay marched over the mountains to Suda, where they embarked in H.M.S. Hero on the night of 26th May. This necessarily abbreviated narrative of their exploits before and after the invasion will be enough to show that the Fleet Air Arm may be proud to include " Crete " among its battle honours.

During the invasion of Crete, the Formidable, the only carrier available, had been operating with the Mediterranean Fleet. On 26th May, after her Albacores and Fulmars had made a successful raid on Scarpanto airfield in the Dodecanese, she was hit twice during an attack by enemy bombers from Libya, and although she was able to proceed to Alexandria under her own steam she could take no further part in the operations. Her squadrons were disembarked to the Western Desert, where the survivors from Crete joined them, to share in that long series of actions by naval aircraft which had begun with the sinking of the Italian warships in Bomba Bay. Thus squadrons from three carriers—the Eagle, the Illustrious and the Formidable—were flying from shore-bases in Libya, and, like those in Malta, supported the varying fortunes of the army in the Middle East until General Montgomery's great advance in October, 1942.

WITH THE EIGHTH ARMY. These two naval officers leave their desert home for an operational flight.

14. DESERT SQUADRONS

LITTLE has been heard of the desert squadrons beyond occasional references in the official communiqués, but their varied activities, carried out night after night, often in bad weather, have, like small contributions to a national fund, proved a most valuable addition to the shore-based air strength of the Allies in the Middle East.

The naval squadrons were not trained, or ever intended, for the work they have had to do, but with the adaptability of seamen the pilots and observers and air-gunners have flown and fought alongside their comrades of the R.A.F. They exchanged the immensity of the sea for the immensity of the desert, where their expert knowledge of navigation has served them well, and the very slowness of their Swordfish and Albacores has enabled them to spot the camouflaged desert targets which faster aircraft might have missed.

At first they sighed for the comforts of their carrier's ante-room, their cabins with hot and cold water, and the good meals which the Ward Room staff provided at any time of the day or night, and they came to realize that hot baths and sound plumbing are not trifling compensations for the rigours of flying at sea. In the desert they found none of these things. They slept in tents which they shared with gregarious flies and desert fleas ; their baths were buckets of water (not much of that) and there was no plumbing. Their messes were made of wood and canvas, which they took pride in making as habitable as possible ; and each had its own bar. Their cooks had to learn the art of cooking meals over open fires, often during a sandstorm. The mainstay of their rations, which they drew from the R.A.F. or the nearest army unit, was bully beef.

The air crews got what sleep they could in he daytime and flew by night. Even when not flying they were at the mercy of the weather, which varied between broiling heat in a shadeless land to deluging rain which transformed the sand into a slough of mud, or sandstorms which filled the aircraft so full of sand that sometimes they could scarcely fly. Such a climate, trying enough to the constitutions both of human beings and of aircraft, is even more trying to the delicate mechanism of torpedoes, and it is to the lasting credit of the naval torpedomen that their weapons seldom failed to run.

The hospitality shown them by the R.A.F. earned their gratitude.

" This good comradeship lasted the whole time we were in the desert," wrote one naval pilot, " and I am sure that it has no small bearing on the efficiency of all concerned. We had a job to do, and whether R.A.F. or F.A.A. did it, made no difference. They lent us transport when they had all too little themselves. They gave us a helping hand with our bombing-up when we were short of men, and we fed in their messes, which must have put a big strain on their small staff—how big we did not appreciate until we were made self-supporting five months later and were given an airfield of our own."

Often the heat in the day-time was so intense that it was impossible to touch the aircraft. Inspections were made at dusk, but only minor repairs were carried out in the desert, the aircraft being sent back for major overhaul to the naval air station in Egypt known as H.M.S. Grebe. This is the headquarters of the Senior Officer, Naval Air Stations, in the Middle East (S.O.N.A.S.), who has administrative control over the shore-based squadrons and works in co-operation with the Air Officer Commanding the R.A.F. In H.M.S. Grebe there is a training squadron for air crews who arrive from home, also a Communications Unit, which provides air transport, and a target-towing section for the use of the Fleet.

Although under the operational control of

DESERT SQUADRON. No carrier and blue waves here, but a sea of sand and dust-laden air. The aircraft are Martlets of the Fleet Air Arm operating in the Western Desert with the Royal Air Force. Protection for the Fleet and convoys was the main job of these shore-based squadrons.

the R.A.F., the desert squadrons worked in close conjunction with the Mediterranean Fleet. When the Libyan campaign began it was the Commander-in-Chief's aim to give as much support to the Army in Egypt as was compatible with his main object : the destruction of the Italian fleet. This support started with spasmodic raids by T.B.R. aircraft on Libyan harbours and occasional sea bombardments, with naval aircraft spotting for gunfire, and grew in intensity during General Wavell's advance in the winter of 1940-1. Naval aircraft guarded the sea route, day and night, carried out anti-submarine patrols, and played havoc with the barges

and lighters in enemy harbours, at the entrances of which mines were adroitly dropped, as well as making numerous night bombing raids in company with the R.A.F.

During this period, and during the withdrawals and advances which followed, the maintenance of the aircraft caused difficulties undreamed of at a home station. Desert warfare travels as swiftly as a desert storm, and the naval air squadrons had to move at short notice from one base to another, the stores and the maintenance parties following as best they could. Nevertheless, thanks to the unflagging efforts of the maintenance ratings, from artificers to mechanics, few aircraft were grounded in those exacting days.

When Rommel's advance had been held up in June, 1942, the work of the desert squadrons did not cease. They dive-bombed the panzer concentrations, landing grounds and ammunition dumps, harried the enemy's lines of communication, and sometimes flew 150 miles out to sea to torpedo a convoy which was bringing him vital reinforcements and supplies. They were the first to give warning of Rommel's short-lived offensive at El Alamein, spotting his armour moving forward, and lighted up the targets while the heavier R.A.F. and American bombers got to work on them. During the Eighth Army's advance they gave the enemy no rest, going out for six hours a night, dive-bombing gun-posts, pounding tanks and transport, moving forward to advanced air-fields, and making themselves indispensable to all three Services, with whom they shared the victory for which they had fought so long. For their part in the attacks the naval airmen received this message from the Air Officer Commanding, Western Desert : " Grand work in the night. By your efforts the enemy is getting no rest, and is suffering heavily by your invaluable share in these most successful air operations." Later, in September, 1942, the A.O.C. made a further signal to the Commander-in-Chief, Mediterranean Fleet : " Please convey to these squadrons my sincere congratulations on their magnificent work with and for the Wellingtons. There is no doubt that these continuous night attacks were one of the decisive factors in crushing the enemy's attack."

The Swordfish and Albacore squadrons in the Western Desert have a long record of fine service and sustained endurance, and the naval fighter squadrons have been operating by their side. Some of the Fulmar squadrons were re-equipped with Hurricanes and their story is that of the Hurricanes, Tomahawks, and Kittyhawks of the R.A.F. Often they flew together. On one occasion Lieutenant-Commander Black was leading a naval Hurricane squadron, flying at 8,000 feet, with a squadron of Tomahawks above, when he met 12 Ju. 87s escorted by 24 Me.109s. There followed what he described as " a tremendous mix up." The Hurricanes and Tomahawks attacked the Ju. 87s. One Hurricane pilot was lost, but another destroyed three of the enemy before he was himself shot down. He landed between the lines of the South Africans and the Italians, but the South Africans reached him first. In all, seven Ju. 87s were destroyed in this foray, and the last Lieutenant-Commander Black saw was "two Messerschmitts knocking hell out of a third."

The main duty of the naval fighters in the Middle East has been to give protection to warships and convoys, and this they have done valiantly, although often outnumbered by aircraft of superior performance. One incident may serve as an example of many.

On 28th December, 1941, a Martlet squadron based near Tobruk was ordered to give protection to an important convoy. One pilot, Sub-Lieutenant (A) A. R. Griffin, R.N.V.R., had trouble with his engine before starting and was left behind. Eventually the defect was remedied and he flew out to sea alone to find the ships. By the time he reached them, the rest of the escort, having completed their patrol, had left the convoy. He was circling over the ships when suddenly he sighted four large Italian torpedo-aircraft coming straight in to attack. Without hesitation he gave battle. He shot down one in flames and forced two more to jettison their torpedoes and make off. The fourth, more determined, was closing in under the heavy barrage from the ships. " Leave him to me," he shouted over his radio. " We are ceasing fire," came the reply. He gave a last shout, " Good show ! " and turned to engage the enemy. The Italian swerved, dropped his torpedo, and missed. Almost simultaneously the Martlet dived headlong into the sea. The pilot and aircraft were lost, but the convoy steamed on undamaged.

TRÖMSO, APRIL, 1940. The carrier Furious is one of the ships giving support to the Army. The ice and slush on her deck give some idea of the difficulties faced by the Fleet Air Arm in operating in these northern latitudes.

15.   IN SUPPORT OF THE ARMY : NORWAY TO MADAGASCAR

NAVAL Aircraft have shown their ability to work with the Merchant Navy across the seas of the world, and with the R.A.F. in Great Britain, Malta and the Middle East. They have also fulfilled another function for which they were not designed—co-operation with military forces on land.

With the opening of the Norwegian campaign in April, 1940, the work of the carriers changed overnight from the unspectacular roles of submarine hunting and trade protection to offensive operations in support of the Norwegian Expeditionary Force. Even when the soldiers ashore did not set eyes on a naval aircraft, the carriers were· in the

background, watchful and vigilant, cruising in dangerous waters within a hundred miles of the coast, their aircraft flying in appalling weather and opposed to an enemy always superior both in performance and in numbers.

The most vital need throughout the campaign was to counter the menace to the Army from the air. This could be done partly by providing fighter protection for the landings and subsequent cover for the troops ashore, and partly by bombing enemy-occupied airfields and other military objectives, and German shipping. The distance from home bases made it impossible for the R.A.F. to provide close fighter protection until landing-grounds in Norway had been improvised, so that the brunt of the defence fell upon the carrier-borne fighters.

On 11th April naval forces escorted the Expeditionary Force to Norway, landings being made at Namsos, Aandalsnes, and near Narvik. On the same day the Furious (Captain T. H. Troubridge, R.N.), the only carrier available, flew off a striking force of Swordfish to attack German cruisers which had been reported at Trondheim. To their disappointment the striking force found nothing more than two small destroyers in the harbour. Owing to shoal water only one possible hit was obtained, but the incident is noteworthy as being the first aircraft torpedo attack of the war.

During the next fortnight the Swordfish were constantly attacking targets afloat and ashore in the Narvik area, bombing destroyers and quays, and enemy aircraft parked on frozen lakes, besides carrying out anti-submarine patrols and photographic reconnaissances. In 14 days the crews flew 23,870 miles, usually in weather that would have daunted any but the most stout-hearted. At times blizzards reduced the ceiling to 250 feet and visibility to a few yards. They had to face the risks of crashing into the high cliffs of the fiords and of turning in rocky ravines no more than a few hundred yards wide. Sometimes, when " ceiling and visibility were zero " as one pilot put it, they were compelled to land in snowdrifts or on frozen fiords. They had to fly over mountainous country without accurate maps, to find their carrier in fog and snow storms, and to land on while the wind was driving across the pitching flight-deck in gusts of over 50 miles an hour. One pilot, after carrying out a low bombing attack on German destroyers in Narvik, had his under-carriage badly damaged by anti-aircraft fire. Although the first of the squadron to return to his ship, he realised the danger of obstructing the flight-deck, and therefore waited one hour in the air before making a perfect landing in the dusk, with one wheel

missing and only a few gallons of petrol in his tank.

" It is difficult to speak without emotion of the pluck and endurance of the young officers and men, some of them midshipmen, who flew their aircraft to such good effect," wrote Captain Troubridge. " Once they had undergone their baptism of fire their morale and spirit rose as each obstacle was in turn successfully surmounted. All were firing their first shot in action, whether torpedo, bomb or machine-gun ; many made their first night landing on 11th April ; and, undeterred by the loss of several of their shipmates, their honour and courage remained throughout as dazzling as the snow-covered mountains over which they so triumphantly flew."

The Furious returned to home waters on 25th April. On the previous day the Ark Royal (Captain, now Rear-Admiral, C. S. Holland), and the Glorious (Captain D'Oyley Hughes, R.N.) had arrived off the Norwegian coast, having been recalled from the Mediterranean. The Ark Royal, which was wearing the flag of Vice-Admiral (now Sir) L. V. Wells, C.B., D.S.O., Vice-Admiral Aircraft-carriers, carried two squadrons of Skuas and two of Swordfish, the Glorious one Skua squadron and one Gladiator squadron, also the R.A.F. Gladiator squadron, which she flew off to a frozen lake on her arrival.

For the next four days these aircraft were employed intensively on patrols over convoys and coastal areas in the neighbourhood of Namsos and Aandalsnes ; they also made raids on ships and seaplanes at anchor in Trondheim harbour and on land targets. They sank nine seaplanes at their moorings, set two tankers on fire, destroyed four hangars and damaged military buildings, and as a result of many air combats they shot down 20 German aircraft and crippled another score. These air combats were sometimes fought at odds of six to one. On one occasion three Skuas brought down a Ju. 88, then attacked three He. 111s,

THE SKUAS STRIKE.   Naval aircraft attacked German supplies and shipping in Norway.   *Left*, A Skua bombs an enemy supply ship at Haugesund.   *Right*, Enemy oil supplies ablaze near Bergen after a Fleet Air Arm attack on 11th May, 1940.

destroying one, then another Ju. 88 without result, and finally eight He.111s. One of these was brought down, and the remainder were forced to jettison their bombs and fled out to sea, two with engines on fire. All three Skuas returned without damage.

After the bombing raid on the seaplane base at Trondheim one of the Skua pilots, Lieutenant A. B. Fraser-Harris, R.N., with his air-gunner, Leading Airman G. Russell, force-landed in a small fiord. The Skua had been badly holed and began to sink rapidly. The dinghy was damaged and impossible to use.   The pilot and the air-gunner were compelled to swim ashore.

" The water was extremely cold, and we had great difficulty in walking up the beach to a group of Norwegians," wrote Lieutenant Fraser-Harris in his official report. " They were very unfriendly, but had mistaken us for German airmen, two of whom they had killed the day before. As soon as our identity was established, their attitude changed completely and we were given warm clothing and food. We were only a short distance from the German forts, and German patrols were on the roads. So, dressed as Norwegians, we were led by a guide to a small farm in the mountains. Shortly after our arrival several Norwegians came in from the vicinity of the

German forts and also from Trondheim. From them I collected what appeared to be valuable and urgent information and decided to try to get through to the British Head-quarters forthwith.

" We travelled in Norwegian dress. A guide who spoke English and who knew the way to the British lines arranged the journey. We left at 2200 and walked to the head of the valley, where we got a sleigh from a farm. On this we travelled for five miles up to a lake in the mountains. Here we left the sleigh, and at 0330 set off on skis up a river valley to the north. Our efforts at this art were not a success, and we finally walked, going being fairly good on the frozen snow. . ."

After eight miles they reached a farm on the other side of the mountains, were given breakfast, left by sleigh at 8 a.m., reached a small valley at the foot of another fiord, and travelled by boat to Folafo, where the Norwegian police found them a taxi.   In this they arrived at the British Brigade Headquarters, having covered 69 miles in 24 hours, and eventually rejoined the Glorious.

After a brief respite the two carriers continued their operations in the Narvik area. Towards the end of May the R.A.F. landing grounds in Norway were completed.   The

Glorious and the Furious transported about thirty Hurricanes and Gladiators from the United Kingdom, flying them off when they reached the Norwegian coast. All three carriers then returned to England for a week.

At the beginning of June the evacuation of Norway began. For the final phase of that unhappy campaign the Ark Royal and the Glorious arrived off Narvik on 3rd June, the Ark to provide fighter protection and security patrols over the troops and transports, the Glorious to re-embark some of the R.A.F. fighters so recently flown ashore. Many of them were flown on by R.A.F. pilots who had had no previous deck-

END OF THE KÖNIGSBERG. Eight Skuas attacked the 6,000-ton German cruiser at Bergen on 10th April, 1940, hitting her three times. Fifty minutes later she sank, the first large enemy warship to be destroyed by air attack

landing experience. When the embarkation was completed the Glorious was detached from the Fleet to return to Scapa, escorted by the destroyers Ardent and Acosta. On the afternoon of 8th June she was intercepted by two heavy German warships believed to be the Scharnhorst and Gneisenau. Outranged, hit by the third salvo and unable to fly off her aircraft, she was sunk by gunfire within forty minutes. In spite of the destroyers' gallant attempts to counter-attack both suffered a like fate. Some days later a merchant ship arrived at Lerwick with some 25 survivors whom she had rescued from Carley floats after 36 hours of great hardship.

During the campaign the catapult aircraft in the cruisers had done valuable work, spotting for bombardments, and making photographic reconnaissances. On 18th May a squadron of Walruses, under Commander R. S. D. Armour, R.N., was established at Harstad, where it carried out anti-submarine and convoy patrols, investigated intelligence reports, and made over 200 communication flights, ferrying British and French naval and military officers in a region where facilities ashore were slow or non-existent (on one of these trips the pilot flew for 12 hours with stops only for refuelling) and made a successful bombing attack on a concentration of German troops at Solfolla. The squadron re-embarked in the Ark Royal on 8th May.

The carrier-borne aircraft had the support of the Skua squadrons which were based in H.M.S. Sparrowhawk in the Orkneys. Flying almost to the limit of their endurance, they made a number of dive-bombing raids on German warships and supply ships and on coastal targets such as fuel tanks and warehouses, sometimes escorted by a section of R.A.F. Blenheim fighters. They made several expeditions to Bergen. They bombed and sank the steamer Bahrenfels alongside the mole, but their most brilliant achievement was on 10th April, when two squadrons, each consisting of eight Skuas, led by

Lieutenant W. P. Lucy, R.N., and Captain R. T. Partridge, R.M., attacked the 6,000-ton German cruiser Königsberg. The Skuas secured three direct hits, one bomb falling squarely amidships between the funnels. Within 50 minutes of the attack the cruiser had capsized and sunk. This was the first large German warship to be sunk by air attack.

With the end of the Norwegian campaign, and the entry of Italy into the war, the main theatre of naval operations shifted to the Mediterranean and North Africa. The manner in which shore-based naval air squadrons supported the military operations has already been described, but co-operation was also given by carrier-borne aircraft. In July striking forces from the Eagle made two very gallant torpedo attacks on shipping at Tobruk, sinking a submarine and damaging several merchant ships. Swordfish from the Ark Royal made several attacks on Elmas airfield in Sardinia ; those from the Illustrious dive-bombed the airfields at Calato and Leros, sank a destroyer and a supply ship at Benghazi and raided Tripoli.

These operations, and there were many more, all furthered the work of the troops ashore. Early in 1941 the land offensive in Italian East Africa began and at times carriers worked in even closer co-operation with the land forces. Before the occupation of Kismayu, in Italian Somaliland, the Navy assisted the two columns which were advancing on the town by bombing and bombarding it. An aircraft from H.M.S. Hermes spotted for the Shropshire's gunfire and carried out a photographic reconnaissance, and between 10th and 19th February her Swordfish forced several Axis supply ships to stop and dropped bags containing previously prepared messages in Italian and German directing them towards H.M.S. Hawkins, which sent armed guards and anti-scuttling parties on board. One German ship was abandoned by her crew on being sighted by the aircraft, and another, carrying white troops, was bombed and damaged. Only one Axis merchantman escaped.

Between 2nd February and 2nd March the Formidable, while on her way round the Cape to join the Mediterranean Fleet, sent out four striking forces to co-operate with the army. The first of these was against Mogadishu, the port north of Kismayu, when mines were laid, followed by a bombing attack by nine Albacores. The remaining attacks were delivered against Massawa in the Red Sea. The objectives were destroyers, submarines, and merchant ships in the harbour. Two attacks were made at night, the third at dawn. The Albacores encountered considerable opposition from gunfire and searchlights. The estimated damage was one merchant ship sunk, and three destroyers, one submarine, one merchant ship and a floating dock damaged.

Shortly before the fall of Massawa 17 of the Eagle's Swordfish, led by Commander C. L. Keighly-Peach, R.N., flew from Alexandria to Port Sudan, covering the distance of 1,200 miles in two days, and ended Italian resistance in the Red Sea by bombing a flotilla of Italian destroyers which, according to an R.A.F. report from Aden, had left Massawa on 2nd April, heading north.

At dawn next morning eight Swordfish were sent out on an armed search. The

DESTRUCTION AT MASSAWA. Shortly before the Red Sea port was entered by the Army on 8th April, 1941, it was attacked by Albacores.

remaining aircraft of the squadron were bombed up and kept in readiness. Commander Keighly-Peach elected to make an independent search off Port Sudan. When he was about ten miles out he saw one of his Swordfish diving towards the sea.

" On following down through the clouds," he wrote, " I saw a lovely fat Italian destroyer right beneath me, and a second later another just zigging away ahead of her. They fired at us extremely ineffectively and after dropping my stick, which fell across the stern of the leading ship without hitting, I made all speed back to Port Sudan to whip up the main party."

From that time the Swordfish shadowed the destroyers and bombed them in relays as fast as the aircraft could get back to refuel and reload. Sub-Lieutenant (A) S. H. Suthers, R.N., dropped two bombs between the funnels of one ship. Her crew abandoned her and she sank an hour later. Midshipman E. Sergeant scored six hits with a stick of six bombs on another. She disappeared in 30 seconds. The remaining two destroyers were found beached and abandoned. They were finally destroyed by H.M.S. Kingston. The fifth destroyer had turned back to Massawa on being sighted and finally scuttled herself in the harbour shortly before the British troops arrived.

H.M.S. Kingston presented the squadron with the Italian ensign from one of the beached destroyers, and it finally went down with the Eagle, flying from a gaff inside the hangar.

At the end of April, 1941, German activities in Iraq forced the British Government to intervene, and although this was almost entirely a land campaign some part was played by naval aircraft from the Hermes, which was recalled from the Indian Ocean to patrol the Persian Gulf. Six of her Swordfish made a demonstration flight over Basra on 3rd May, and on the 7th, owing to the distance of the carrier from the sphere of action, a small striking force was based ashore at Shaibah under the operational control of

Air Officer Commanding, Iraq. Between 4th and 16th May ten dive-bombing attacks were made on railway bridges, petrol and oil tanks, barracks, and troop concentrations. The rifle and automatic fire of the Iraqi irregulars was extremely accurate and several aircraft were hit. One was compelled to come down near the barracks at Samawa and was immediately surrounded by Iraqis, who opened fire as they approached. Seeing this, the leader of the striking force, Lieutenant J. H. Dundas, R.N., made a difficult landing alongside the damaged Swordfish, and by a feat of great daring and consummate airmanship, succeeded in taking off again with the stranded crew in spite of the heavy small-arms fire, the appalling ground surface, and the double load.

Naval aircraft also took part in the Syrian campaign, attacking ships at sea and in harbour with bombs and torpedoes. On the night of 16th June, 1941, five Swordfish, armed with torpedoes, were sent out to intercept a Vichy destroyer, the Chevalier Paul, which was known to be rushing reinforcements to Syria from Salonika. At 3 a.m., one of the Swordfish found the destroyer steaming at high speed to the northward of Cyprus. Two of the other searchers joined in the attack, hitting the Chevalier Paul in the boiler room and bringing her to a stop. This was a re-markable feat—to hit a small vessel, travelling at least 35 knots, at night. One of the Swordfish failed to return. Next morning three Swordfish went out to discover the position of the ship, which was believed to be only damaged. They found nothing but wreckage, empty boats and an empty Sword-fish dinghy. It transpired later that two other French destroyers had gone to the rescue of the Chevalier Paul (which had sunk soon after being hit) and had picked up the survivors, including the pilot and observer of the crashed Swordfish, who were eventually repatriated in exchange for French prisoners of war taken in the campaign.

Thus, in a number of widely distant campaigns, naval aircraft were able to give support to the land forces. It was not until the occupation of Madagascar, however, that co-operation became more fully developed, and this was but the rehearsal for even more important operations elsewhere.

To prevent the enemy from obtaining a naval base for attacking convoys in the Mozambique Channel it became necessary to seize Diego Suarez, at the extreme north of the island, and the neighbouring town of Antsirane. Operations began on 5th May, 1942. The Expeditionary Force was commanded by Major-General R. G. Sturges, C.B., R.M. Vice-Admiral E. N. Syfret was in command of the naval covering force, flying his flag in H.M.S. Ramillies. As in the Norwegian campaign, the Navy provided fighter and T.B.R. aircraft to protect and assist the advancing troops. The two carriers present were the Illustrious (Captain A. G. Talbot, D.S.O., R.N.), and the Indomitable (Captain T. H. Troubridge, R.N.) wearing the flag of Rear-Admiral D. W. Boyd, Commanding Aircraft-Carriers, Eastern Fleet.

The relations between the naval air squadrons and the Army could not have been better. "All the preliminary discussions," wrote Captain Talbot, "were characterised by a genuine desire to help each other to the full."

Profiting by the experience gained in the Norwegian campaign, nothing was left to chance. Detailed operation orders were issued, and by means of maps of the island, Admiralty charts, and photographs taken by the South African Air Force, relief models of Diego Suarez and Antsirane were made for each carrier, to enable the flying crews to recognise the countryside in varying lights.

At dawn on 5th May, a striking force of Albacores from the Indomitable bombed the airfield and set the hangar on fire. While her fighters kept the French aircraft grounded and attacked the .75 batteries, those from the Illustrious gave cover to the transports and the landing parties. Shortly before 4 a.m. the Illustrious flew off three striking forces, each composed of six Swordfish. The first,

armed with torpedoes, attacked the sloop D'Entrecasteaux, without results, then torpedoed the armed merchant cruiser Bougainville, which blew up. The second striking force, carrying depth-charges, sank the submarine Bevezières, and the third, having dropped leaflets and copies of an ultimatum to the Governor, bombed a gun battery and then the sloop D'Entrecasteaux. The leader of this striking force, Lieutenant R. N. Everett, R.N., had his engine hit by anti-aircraft fire during his last bombing run and was forced to land in the sea near one of the beaches. He and his crew were taken prisoner, but were released after the occupation of Antsirane.

Later in the morning another Swordfish bombed the sloop, which had got under way. One bomb penetrated to the platform deck and exploded, with the result that the vessel had to be beached. Three Swordfish completed her destruction. After the occupation her bell, which had been holed by a .303 bullet, was secured by one of the Indomitable's squadrons as a trophy.

The Martlets patrolled the beaches throughout the next day. Some carried out tactical reconnaissances for the Army, and kept watch over the town and the anchorage. Others were used for ground-strafing enemy positions which were holding up the advance. At 6 a.m. the patrolling fighters sighted three Potez 63 bombers, one of which bombed the approaches to the town, while the other two made for the transports. The Martlets shot down all three without loss to themselves.

On the morning of 7th May the Martlet patrol saw two Morane fighters approaching from the south-west. The leader of the section attacked the first Morane head on. His aircraft was hit in the wings and the engine, and he forced-landed in the water off one of the beaches. For two days he was presumed missing, but he was in fact unhurt, and had made his way ashore; he eventually embarked in another ship. Meanwhile the second Martlet had followed his leader into the attack, but seeing two more Moranes following him he turned and shot down one of them. The pilots of the Martlet section which was flying above as top cover, seeing the dog-fight below them, dived and shot down the remaining three Moranes. The leader, Lieutenant (A) C. C. Tomkinson, R.N.V.R. (who had accounted for a Potez on the previous day) destroyed one, Sub-Lieutenant (A) J. Waller, R.N.V.R., bringing down the other two. By the time a supporting range of four Martlets from the Illustrious arrived on the scene the sky was clear of French fighters.

As a result of the three days' fighting seven enemy aircraft were shot down for the loss of one Martlet, and the troops had been given complete protection from air attack. The carriers also performed a number of specific tasks for the Army, such as bombing points of enemy resistance and creating diversions. One Swordfish spotted during the destroyer Laforey's bombardment of gun emplacements south of Antsirane. Another, piloted by Sub-Lieutenant (A) F. H. Alexander, R.N.V.R., sank the submarine La Héros with depth-charges. As the submarine began to go down after being blown to the surface, the pilot observed the crew taking to the sea. He led a corvette to the spot, with the result that four officers and thirty-one ratings were rescued.

The town and the naval base capitulated on 8th May. The moral effect of the naval air superiority had been as heartening to the British troops as it had been discouraging to the enemy, who believed that the naval squadrons had 150 aircraft in the sky.

" We went into this operation without being fully worked up," wrote Captain Talbot. " We came out of it having had a real belly-full. From the air-operational, the deck-handling, the maintenance, in fact from every point of view, the experience was invaluable. Further, every flying crew was ' blooded,' although in most cases it was only by light anti-aircraft fire. Although the operation only lasted four days, the strain on the flight-deck personnel and the flying staff

FIRST DAY IN MADAGASCAR. Parachutes are dropping over Madagascar from naval aircraft on 5th May, 1942, when the Madagascar campaign began. As in Norway, the Fleet Air Arm protected and helped the advancing troops.

was considerable, there being little, if any, opportunity for sleep."

During the six months which followed before the end of French resistance the naval air squadrons had a long and arduous task. They were used mainly for reconnaissance and performed valuable service in the assault on the final positions. Their superiority in the air was hardly challenged, even by anti-aircraft fire, but the crews, based ashore far from their carriers and working in conjunction with the South African Air Force, were in constant danger from the mist-covered mountains and had to fly from very rough landing-grounds. Their bombing shattered the morale of the enemy, particularly the native troops, and the air-gunners scared the transport from the roads. When the supply of bombs ran short they dropped empty beer bottles from the sky—full ones being too precious. These whistled down with a frightening shriek and helped to demoralise the enemy. But, as one of the Press correspondents on the spot observed, it was " as the eyes of the troops that the airmen were superb." Throughout the campaign the maintenance parties manhandled the cumbersome transport over scores of rivers and broken bridges, sleeping at night under the aircraft or on rain-sodden landing grounds.

Many of the tasks which the Fleet Air Arm were called upon to perform would have been considered beyond the scope of naval aircraft even a year previously, but it had come to be realized that the success of combined operations carried out far from airfields ashore could be ensured only by the aircraft carriers giving support to the troops on the ground. It was the proper understanding of this function of the Fleet Air Arm which sealed the success of the greater operation to follow in North Africa, which the First Lord of the Admiralty then described as the greatest amphibious expedition of all time.

16.   THE SHAPE OF THINGS TO COME : NORTH AFRICA

FOR the great task ahead, weeks of previous preparation were necessary in the carriers alone. Much of this work fell on the Paymasters' departments, which are responsible not only for the provision of food and equipment for the whole ship's company, but also for the supply of the countless accessories and spare parts for the aircraft. This duty entails immense forethought and precision, for once the carrier has put to sea it is too late to remedy a shortage, or requisition for any essential part that has been left behind.

As Vice-Admiral Lyster has said, " An aircraft is rendered entirely useless perhaps more easily than any other comparable piece of machinery." There are many ways of repairing and remedying defects to a ship. There is no substitute for a burst tyre in an aircraft except a new one. If no spares are available when required, the aircraft is useless. It can only feed like a cannibal upon its fellows, which have to be pulled to pieces and made unserviceable in their turn. Stores are thus the very life-blood of a carrier, so that she can maintain, in all the adversities of battle, the limited number of aircraft she can carry.

No reserves can be drawn upon, as in the R.A.F., and consequently maintenance of the highest standard is a more pressing need for carrier-borne aircraft than for shore-based squadrons. This applies also to aircraft armament. Shortly before one of the carriers sailed, certain essential armament tools were found to be lacking one Saturday afternoon. A telephone call was put through to the Managing Director of the firm which provided them. He said that all his work people had gone for the week-end, but volunteered to go to the benches himself and turn out twenty sets of the required tools. This he did, and the tools were despatched on the following Monday afternoon.

Besides all this, there was the training of the air crews. As at Madagascar, models of the objectives were made from photographic mosaics, and maps were carefully prepared ; each squadron was given elaborate briefing on its task.

Several aircraft carriers were to be employed, including some of the new escort carriers from the United States. Some embarked Seafires, a " navalized " type of the incomparable Spitfire armed with two 20 mm. cannon. (The first Seafire squadron to land on a carrier—the Furious—was that commanded by Lieutenant A. B. Fraser-Harris, D.S.C., R.N.) Others had Sea-Hurricanes, which had made their first appearance in the Mediterranean in June. There were also Martlet, Fulmar and Albacore squadrons, and a small number of Swordfish for anti-submarine patrols. Thus, with the Walruses carried in the capital ships and cruisers, every type of naval aircraft in operation was represented.

The Commander-in-Chief of the Allied Forces was Lieutenant-General Dwight D. Eisenhower of the United States Army. Admiral Sir Andrew Cunningham commanded the naval forces. These were divided into three squadrons : the Western Naval Task Force, composed entirely of American ships and carriers, whose objective was Casablanca ; the Central Naval Task Force, under the command of Commodore T. H. Troubridge, R.N., destined for Oran ; and the Eastern Naval Task Force, under the command of Rear-Admiral Sir Harold Burrough, bound for Algiers. A high military officer of the United States Army and his Staff sailed with the Admiral of each Task Force. The naval commander had full control until the troops in the assault convoy had landed, when the military leaders took over. The dividing line of authority was the beach.

Covering the landings at Oran and Algiers was Force H, composed of battleships, cruisers, a large number of destroyers and two Fleet carriers, one of which wore the flag of Rear-Admiral A. L. St. G. Lyster. Force H was commanded by Vice-Admiral Sir Neville Syfret. Its mission was to protect the Central and Eastern Task Forces from interference by either the French or Italian fleets. Each of the carriers had on board American liaison officers and radio telegraphists.

The date appointed for the landings was 8th November. This was officially referred to as D—the Day. The great Expeditionary Force passed through the Straits on the 6th (D–2). Hudsons and Sunderlands from Gibraltar took over the anti-submarine patrols. On D–1 the carriers sent up fighter patrols over the convoy and Force H. No enemy aircraft were seen until the fighters shot down a Potez 63, which they intercepted

10,000 feet above Force H. Otherwise it was a quiet day—perfect Mediterranean weather, no cloud, a light wind.

A shadower, espying those long columns of merchant ships steaming to the eastward, might well have supposed that the Fleet was escorting yet another convoy to Malta ; and it is now known that the Axis Powers were completely deceived. But during the night, at an appointed time, all the ships turned towards the North African coast, the Central Force to Oran, the Eastern Force to Algiers. The assault convoys were in position by 11 p.m. Zero hour was 1 a.m. on the 8th. Force H remained in the background, some distance from the Algerian coast.

The smaller carriers were closer inshore. Their task was to fly off their fighters at first light to give cover to the transports and to patrol the landing beaches. They met with no opposition.

Enemy aircraft found Force H, however, about 4 a.m. They dropped flares for about an hour, but strangely enough there was no attack. By five o'clock reports began to come in that the landings had been successful, and half an hour later two Albacores from one of the Fleet carriers were flown off for anti-submarine patrols round Force H, and three more to stop vessels from breaking out of the harbour and to " smell along the beaches " for U-boats that might be lurking to attack the transports. As they roared over the beaches, the air crews had their first sight of the landing ships and smaller landing craft which were still putting ashore the assault forces for an operation that was the culmination of long planning, meticulous organization, and months of special combined training.

By 5.45 the sky began to lighten. Four Martlets were sent to patrol over the military airfield at Blida, 30 miles south-west of Algiers. The pilots' orders were to prevent French aircraft leaving the ground and to attack any they saw moving. When they reached the airfield they observed two aircraft preparing to take off, and gave them some machine-gun fire. The movement ceased. They encountered some light anti-aircraft opposition, but there was no other activity.

They returned to their carrier, and at 8 a.m. another section of four Martlets was flown off to continue the patrol. After circling the airfield for half an hour the leader, Lieutenant (A) B. H. C. Nation, R.N., noticed people waving white handkerchiefs. Peasants in the surrounding fields were also waving. Lieutenant Nation reported this by R/T to his carrier, but at first the staff was dubious that the French were ready to surrender. Was he sure that he was over the right airfield? Quite sure, he replied; there was an enormous circle on the ground with BLIDA in big white letters.

Since the land campaign was under American control, Rear-Admiral Lyster then offered to have his Liaison Officer, Captain Hanson, U.S. Army, flown off to accept the surrender of the airfield. Captain Hanson asked that the honour should go to the Fleet Air Arm. Lieutenant Nation was then told that he might detail one pilot to land. He decided to go down himself, telling his three pilots to keep watch above him.

He landed without mishap, and taxied his Martlet to the hangars, where a group of

THE GREAT EXPEDITIONARY FORCE steams majestically towards Africa.

French officers awaited him. They took him to the Station Commandant, a French General ("a nice old boy and very friendly"), who immediately tore a piece of paper off his writing pad, seized a pen and scribbled these words :

"La base de Blida est disponible pour l'atterissage des armées alliés "—" Blida base is at the disposal of the Allied armies for landing purposes."

This document he dated and signed, then handed it to Lieutenant Nation, who was somewhat embarrassed at having a large airfield thrust upon his hands. The Fighter School at H.M.S. Heron had taught him no drill for such an emergency. He behaved, however, with that aplomb which is the birthright of naval officers who find themselves in peculiar circumstances, and remained in amiable converse with the French officers until (to his relief) a party of Commandos and Rangers arrived. Then, having handed over his charge (but retaining the document) he took off, joined his section which was still waiting for him overhead, and returned to his ship.

The Royal Navy is a kindly service, and no one had the heart to deprive him, even for official records, of the declaration of surrender. It was photographed and returned

to him and, no doubt, will be handed down to his descendants, neatly framed, like the swords and ensigns surrendered to naval officers of an older day.

During this little interlude the fighters had been patrolling over the civil airport of Algiers, known as Maison Blanche, of which the landing forces had taken control by the time the Martlets arrived. The carrier-borne aircraft were able to make use of it throughout the day, and, later, R.A.F. squadrons from Gibraltar moved in.

As part of the plan for co-operation between the naval aircraft and the troops ashore a Fulmar squadron, commanded by Captain R. C. Hay, D.S.C., R.M., had been specially trained in tactical reconnaissance at an Army Co-operation School before embarking. Immediately after the first Martlet had been flown off, two Fulmars set out to reconnoitre the roads leading to Algiers. They observed no movements of troops, but the peasants in the fields and the villages waved to them as they passed overhead. These reconnaissances were made every few hours and on the following days were extended to a radius of 100 miles from Algiers. The Fulmars also carried out contact patrols to identify the forward positions of the landing forces.

The Albacore squadrons also had their share in the operations. To prevent sabotage in the harbour and the scuttling of merchant ships, two destroyers had been detailed to crash through the boom. After some difficulty one succeeded in forcing an entrance, but met with considerable resistance from the batteries in the naval forts, particularly one on the Jetée du Nord. The F.A.A. received a request for assistance, and six Albacores, which had been ranged in readiness for such a call, flew off and bombed the fort. The guns were silenced. Before the striking force had landed back on the ship another request was received to bomb Fort du Perré, on an escarpment to the westward of Algiers, overlooking the sea, which was holding out against the Commandos. A second striking force of Albacores, armed

ESCORTS FOR THE CONVOY, the carriers Avenger

press on through stormy weather. Fighters are ranged on the pitching flight-decks.

with bombs, quickly silenced the fort, which capitulated to the troops. About the same time another Albacore squadron was dealing equally successfully with the naval outpost of Fort Matifou.

Towards evening the carriers off Algiers moved inshore to within four miles of the coast. About 5 p.m., as dusk was approaching, one sent up a patrol of three Seafires. While they were still climbing they sighted 15 Ju. 88s, flying at 20,000 feet. Before the Seafires could get height to attack, the enemy dived on their carrier. Another three Seafires were ranged on the flight-deck, the pilots sitting in the cockpits, but when the attack came the carrier had not yet turned back into wind, so that they could not be flown off. The Junkers came down to 500 feet and bombed the ship for four minutes. There were several near misses, and the last bomb hit the port quarter, blowing off the tail of the Seafire ranged on the port side of the flight-deck and damaging the others with blast. None of the pilots was hurt. The three who were still in the air landed at Maison Blanche and returned to the carrier on the following day.

A formation of Ju. 88s also attacked Force H at dusk on 8th November, but it was a half-hearted attempt and caused no damage. Indeed, throughout the operation there was no sign of the heavy air assaults upon the Fleet which had been so characteristic of previous operations in the Mediterranean, and enemy air activity near Force H usually took the form of an armed reconnaissance twice daily by Ju. 88s flying singly at a great height and carrying only one bomb.

While the carriers were operating in this way off Algiers, aircraft from the others were performing similar duties off Oran. Seven miles inland from Oran is a large salt-lake, twelve miles long and one mile wide. At the north-eastern corner, immediately south of Oran, is the military airfield of La Senia. The civil airport, Tafaraoui, is five miles to the south again.

At daylight on 8th November a striking force of Albacores, led by Lieutenant (A) J. G. A. McI. Nares, R.N., was sent out with an escort of Seafires and Hurricanes. The fighters passed over the airfields at 8,000 feet without sighting any enemy in the air, then descended and carried out low-flying attacks. The Seafires encountered both heavy and light anti-aircraft fire, but silenced several of the guns. The aircraft of Lieutenant Fraser-Harris, the Squadron Commander, was hit ; he forced-landed, set fire to his aircraft, and was taken prisoner, being released when the American armoured column entered the town. The squadron was also attacked by a number of Dewoitine 520 fighters. Sub-Lieutenant (A) G. C. Baldwin, D.S.C., R.N., shot down one, which crashed a mile east of La Senia airfield. This was the Seafires' first victim. Several others were hit and damaged.

Following the fighters, the Albacore striking force, led by Lieutenant Nares, with an escort of Hurricanes, dropped leaflets over the Valmy area, then bombed La Senia airfield and destroyed 47 aircraft in hangars and dispersed on the ground. During the Albacores' run in, the whole squadron was subjected to intense anti-aircraft fire and to attacks by Dewoitine fighters, but all reached the target although some were already damaged. Lieutenant Nares actually attacked in flames. Although he could have baled out, he did not do so, but went on to his objective, and to certain death.

As the Albacores dived a number of Dewoitines got on their tails. The Hurricanes shot down five Dewoitines without loss, and an air-gunner in one of the Albacores destroyed another. Four Albacores were lost, including the leader, but of three, the crews were saved. Two pilots and one observer were wounded. The bombing was extremely accurate and accounted for the troops' complete immunity from air attack.

Meanwhile other aircraft were on reconnaissance, dropping leaflets and creating diversions. Some went at intervals to report

READY FOR THE ENEMY FLEET that never came, Force H, with carriers bearing strong forces of modern naval aircraft, is covering the landings at Oran and Algiers. In the foreground Seafires await the call to action.

on the situation in Oran harbour. Three of the pilots flew to the limit of their endurance and forced-landed. One was picked up from the sea ; the others, who landed near the beach, obtained petrol from the troops and returned to the ship next morning.

After the striking force had returned from bombing La Senia airfield, a tactical reconnaissance of five Seafires was sent out with four to provide top cover. While the reconnaissance force was examining the road between La Senia and Lourmel airfields the fighter cover was attacked by seven Dewoitines, one of which was shot down. Sub-Lieutenant (A) L. P. Twiss, D.S.C., R.N.V.R., having completed his reconnaissance of the La Senia—Lourmel road, landed alongside an American tank column, climbed out of his cockpit and asked the Commanding Officer if he could help

in any way. The Tank Commander was delighted, and asked him to reconnoitre the roads running to the south-west and south-east. He saw no movement of troops, and landed again alongside the tanks to report. By this time he was too short of petrol to return to the ship, so he took a chance and landed at Tafaraoui, which he believed, but was not certain, had been captured ; actually the French were still moving out. On landing he broke his tail-wheel but, having found a crashed aircraft, he removed its tail-wheel and repaired his own, filled up with petrol from another wrecked aircraft, and after sleeping the night under the wing of his Seafire, took off next morning and landed on his carrier.

Similar operations continued on the following day (D+1), both at Algiers and Oran. A new landing was made at Bougie

BLIDA AIRFIELD SURRENDERS. To a naval
pilot, landing by himself, the commandant of Blida
airfield handed these scribbled words: " Blida base is at
the disposal of the Allied armies for landing purposes."

Beach, to the east of Algiers, and Seafires
patrolled the beaches. Reconnaissance and
fighter patrols were kept over Oran. The
Albacores bombed a battery of artillery with
good results. One Hurricane, coming in to
land on its carrier, missed the deck and
dived into the sea 200 yards ahead of the
ship. The aircraft sank in ten seconds, but
the pilot bobbed up unhurt. Another pilot
crashed on deck, leapt out of the cockpit and
ran up to the bridge where he reported
excitedly to the captain, " I shot one down,
sir." The Commanding Officer eyed the
wrecked Hurricane. " One all, then," he
said.

By the 9th, American-flown Spitfires from
Gibraltar had occupied Tafaraoui airfield,
and with those at Algiers also in their hands
the main work of the Fleet Air Arm was done.
The capitulation of Oran on the 10th fore-
stalled a dive-bombing attack by Albacores
against its forts. Some of the carriers
returned to Gibraltar, others remained to
give cover to the troops ashore and to the
subsequent convoys. By that time the U-
boats had massed their forces, and Force H
kept up anti-submarine sweeps on three
successive nights. An Albacore torpedoed a
submarine, and a Walrus from one of the
cruisers picked up two " token survivors."
The patrols were maintained on the return

passage from Gibraltar, but could not save
one of the small escort carriers, the Avenger,
(Captain A. P. Colthurst, R.N.), from being
torpedoed and sunk at night.

" The operations of the aircraft-carriers
went according to plan," wrote Rear-
Admiral Lyster in his official despatch, and
added, " After such great effort to re-equip
nearly all the naval squadrons with modern
fighters in time for this operation, disappointment has been expressed that the
enemy were not sufficiently attentive to
Force H."

It was but natural that the fighter pilots
should have hoped to have had more
combats ; some did not fire their guns.
For months they had been clamouring for
cannon and for increased speed ; now that
they had cannon there had been nothing to
shoot and some of them felt that they had
been wasting their fleetness on the desert
air. Unspectacular though it may have been,
however, the operation was a most significant
development in the capabilities of the Fleet
Air Arm, and, with the exception of torpedo-
dropping and spotting for gunfire, the
flying crews had performed every function
proper to naval aircraft, and some—such as
tactical reconnaissance by fighters—which
were new.

The organization and the timing had been
perfect. The aircraft, like the troops, had the
supreme advantage of surprise, and, as at
Madagascar, the naval air superiority was
scarcely challenged. The Fleet Air Arm had
been able to protect the assault convoys and
the landing parties on the beaches. It had
always had a striking force of Albacores
available to launch a torpedo attack should
either the French or Italian fleet come out.
It had paved the way for the capture of the
all-important airfields, thereby enabling
the shore-based squadrons to take over. It
had provided anti-submarine patrols for
the ships of Force H and the Task Forces.
By keeping the French Air Force grounded
it had saved the troops from the perils of
dive-bombing or machine-gunning from the

air. It had reconnoitred the countryside for the Army and, when the military advance was held up, it had bombed strongly fortified positions into speedy submission.

The time is not yet ripe to tell the full story of the Expeditionary Force's landings in North Africa, and this account has necessarily been restricted to the part played by the carriers and the naval aircraft. That part had been to give the assault troops all possible support from the air, and they had performed it faithfully and gallantly, thus contributing to the success of those momentous operations which were, as time has shown, but the prelude to even greater things to come.

"THE OPERATIONS OF THE AIRCRAFT-CARRIERS WENT ACCORDING TO PLAN."
A Martlet of the Fleet Air Arm, bearing American markings, flies off a British carrier during the African operations, while other Martlets and Seafires are ready to follow. The Fleet Air Arm protected the Fleet and transports, covered the landings, and supported the advance.

SINCE the outbreak of War the Fleet Air Arm has increased in power like a rising wind : a wind that has swept all the seas of the world. Naval aircraft have ranged the oceans in search of raiders and U-boats ; they have guarded the paths of seaborne trade ; they have protected the Fleet. They have attacked German and Italian warships—from battleships to submarines—under steam and in defended harbours, and have sunk more than half a million tons of merchant shipping. They were the first aircraft in history to sink a warship by dive-bombing, the first to sink a capital ship with torpedoes, and the first to defeat air attack on a fleet by fighter defence.

Often they have been the first to report enemy forces at sea, and, by shadowing them and crippling them with their torpedoes, have enabled the Admiral to bring them to action. Flying from frozen airfields and desert landing grounds, or from their carriers' decks, they have caused untold damage to ports, airfields, factories and fortifications, transport on road and rail. Under the cover of night they have sown mines in estuaries and harbours. They have marked the gunfire of the Fleet. They have lent their aid to expeditionary forces ashore. Their sphere of action has known no limits between Petsamo and the Falklands. They have flown the Pacific and the Indian oceans, and in destroying two Japanese bombers off Ceylon they struck their first blow against a third enemy.

Their numbers have not been great. For the first three years of the war their pilots had to fight an enemy who had greater speed and better guns. Skill and courage their crews have never lacked ; and now that they are being given modern aircraft and powerful cannon the Axis will have even greater cause to fear them.

As the aircraft have changed, so have the men who fly them. In the beginning the pilots, observers, and telegraphist-air-gunners were drawn from the Royal Navy and the Royal Marines. Many of them gave their lives. Some are still flying ; some have risen to higher commands ; others are using their experience to train those who are to follow them. These new air crews are not seamen by profession. They are men who have left school or trade or office to " ride the skies in the service of the Fleet." They have come under naval discipline later in life than those whose ranks they fill, but when they embark in their carriers they are as highly trained ; nor are they slow to accept the tradition and custom of the Service they have joined. Yet they have this difference ; they are a cross-section of the British people who have come from a thousand walks of life to turn their hands to war.

They are at sea because they want to be at sea ; they fly because they want to fly. But their outlook is different from that of the men who flew with the Fleet in the last war, when flying was more romantic than it is to-day. These young men tackle the work they have in hand more seriously, with grim determination. This does not mean that they are not light of heart ; their nerves are such that, when they leave their cockpits after a dog-fight above the Fleet, they will light a cigarette with fingers that do not tremble. Some of them, who have already been through much, have learnt the shining certainty that they will never be afraid. But they have no illusions. They have the measure of the foe they fight. Once, war in the air was a tournament of chivalry. It is so no longer. It is not easy to feel chivalrous to an enemy who drops bombs upon the rescuers of his allies, who machine-guns sailors struggling in the sea.

They are the marines of the sky : airmen and seamen too ; and although they are the hub of the carrier's life they are mindful not only of their maintenance ratings, but of all those others who help the air crews to fight : the Staff Officers who plan operations and direct the squadrons to the enemy ; the paymasters and writers who provide them with stores and spares ; the seamen who range the aircraft ; the signalmen and wireless operators who receive their reports ; the engineers and the stokers below decks ; the cooks and stewards who have a hot meal ready for them when they land on after hours in the air ; the gunners who put a barrage over the ship ; and the Royal Marines who man part of the carrier's armament and play her into harbour when the battle is over.

" Let us show ourselves to be all of a company," Drake exhorted his men in the Golden Hind. This they do, yet at the same time they are a company within a company, and share the intimacy of the air squadron to which they belong. They look to their leader as seamen look to the Bridge, and thus they form a fellowship born of danger shared.

Such are the men upon whose quickness of brain and upon whose swiftness of action the safety of the Fleet, or of a convoy, may depend. Some of their names have been recorded in this book ; for each there is a score of others with equal claims upon their country's gratitude. The decorations they have won are but part of the measure of their glory. If they remain here anonymous, their comrades will remember them. They would have it so. They are not given to speaking of themselves. The Navy has taught them modesty. During the ebb and flow of talk in Ward Rooms afloat and ashore will come a mention of this action or of that, but it is always of someone else they speak, someone who was " the finest pilot I ever knew," or " a wizard observer," or " the best air-gunner I ever had."

This brief account of their achievement is a tribute to those

> Wide eyes that weary never,
> And wings that search the sea.

They are members of the youngest branch of the Royal Navy, which is very old and very wise. Those who led the way have shown what naval aircraft can do, and the future of the Navy in the air is safe in the hands of those who follow them. With new carriers, and at last new aircraft that they may indeed be proud to fly, they shall " ascend and come like a storm " and so pass from victory to victory.

"It is upon the navy,

under the good providence of god, that the wealth

safety and strength of the kingdom do chiefly depend"